Ethno-Logic

Ethno-Logic

The Anthropology of Human Reasoning

James F. Hamill

UNIVERSITY OF ILLINOIS PRESS
Urbana and Chicago

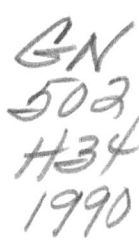
GN
502
H34
1990

Publication of this work was made possible in part by a grant from the College of Arts and Science, Miami University, Oxford, Ohio.

© 1990 by the Board of Trustees of the University of Illinois
Manufactured in the United States of America
C 5 4 3 2 1

This book is printed on acid-free paper.

Library of Congress Cataloging-in-Publication Data
Hamill, James F. (James Francis), 1942–
    Ethno-logic : the anthropology of human reasoning / James F. Hamill.
      p. cm.
    Includes bibliographical references.
    ISBN 0-252-01714-5 (alk. paper)
    1. Ethnopsychology. 2. Logic—Cross-cultural studies. 3. Cognition and culture. 4. Language and culture. 5. Navajo Indians—Psychology. I. Title.
GN502.H34   1990
155.8—dc20   89-48194
                                                                   CIP

To Ward Weakly

Contents

List of Tables   ix

Preface   xi

Introduction   1

1. Meaning, Logic, and Culture   8
2. The Ethnographic Basis of Ethno-Logic   22
3. The Use of Error in the Study of Meaning   44
4. Meaning and Pattern in Syllogisms   60
5. Propositional Reasoning and Navajo Subject Pronouns   73
6. Propositional Reasoning and Navajo Syntactic Time   90
7. Logical Processes in the General Theory of Culture   102

References Cited   113

Index   121

Tables

2-1 Examples of Premise Changes 38
2-2 Lexical/Semantic Universals 42
3-1 Constituent Order and Gapping 53
3-2 Gapping Types by Language 54
4-1 Syllogism Figures 63
4-2 Valid Syllogisms 63
4-3 Lexicon Structure 64
4-4 Protocol Sentences 64
4-5 Protocol Sentence Combinations 65
4-6 Syllogism Test Categories 66
4-7 Hypothetical Categories 67
4-8 Invalidly Rejected Conclusions 69
5-1 Navajo Test Propositions 78
5-2 Navajo Obligatory Subject Pronouns 79
5-3 "Or," "If . . . Then" Test Design 79
5-4 "And" Test Design 80
5-5 *Áádóó* ("And") Test Results 82
5-6 *Diégo* ("If . . . Then") Test Results 83
5-7 *Éédoodaii'* ("Or") Test Results 84
6-1 Navajo Sentential Conjoiners 91
6-2 Navajo Time Markers 91
6-3 "Radical" Translation of English "And" 94
6-4 Logics Exhibited by Navajo Conjoiners 94
6-5 The Logic of Navajo Conjoiners
    with Respect to Syntactic Time Markers 96

Preface

"Ethno-logic" is a word I use to describe the anthropology I practice. It concerns how people think in both universal and culture-specific terms. I am not the first (nor will I be the last) anthropologist to approach this topic; therefore, I rely on previous research. To my knowledge none of the scholars to whom I refer here use "ethno-logic" as a term, so I apologize in advance for painting them with my brush. I will, however, continue to use the term because it captures the interests of researchers who are investigating issues in human reasoning.

One of the important issues in my present and previous work in ethno-logic is the distinction between universal and particular aspects of culture. This distinction highlights the fact that people share a humanity in spite of the diversity of ways of life. Maintaining the distinction is difficult sometimes because anthropologists use the same word—"culture"—to refer to both levels. To avoid this pitfall, some write "culture" with an uppercase C when referring to the universal and a lowercase c when referring to the particular.

This solution, however, does not work very well when the word "culture" is in the sentence initial position or when it occurs in spoken language. Also, although this device is useful because it implies that the universal is part of all particular contexts, it unfortunately may cloud the relationship between the universal and the particular. It ignores the possibility that both universal and particular cultural phenomena are equally derivatives of the same underlying human nature. Because I want to keep this possibility in mind, I will not use the "big C/little c" convention here. I will try to distinguish the universal from the particular only when the distinction is important.

Ethno-Logic: The Anthropology of Human Reasoning is about the way people reason. Reasoning is a kind of knowledge about valid ways to manipulate symbols. It makes little difference whether people apply this knowledge in conscious, overt problem-solving, which is often called reasoning, or in other kinds of thought processes, for example daydreaming or passive observation. People use reasoning whether or not they are aware of it. Accordingly, I can see little distinction between "reasoning" and "thinking," and I will use these two words interchangeably throughout this book.

Reasoning, or thinking, takes place in the creative, self-aware mind, and when people reason, they do so immediately and in real time. Reason consists of arranging information into valid structures or patterns, which often produce new knowledge. Validity refers to the quality of the patterns. Conclusions follow from valid, well-formed patterns, and they do not follow from invalid, ill-formed patterns. If conclusions followed from all the imaginable ways of putting together the information people know, there would be no justification for any configuration; in other words, not putting together (or nonsense) would be one of the valid ways of putting together. Reasoning must be patterned, and some possible patterns must be unreasonable.

I devote the first three chapters of the book to issues of theory and method. In Chapter 1, I establish meaning structures as the analytic focus of the book. Chapter 2 places ethno-logic in its historical context through a review of classic and modern research. Chapter 3 discusses the importance of error in the study of ethno-logical systems and its use in ethno-logical research.

I make use of original research data throughout the work, but most heavily in Chapters 4, 5, and 6, where I show that syllogisms vary little with culture but that propositional patterns change from one cultural setting to another. Chapter 4 reports the results of research that uses the syllogism as the basis for study. The research reported in Chapters 5 and 6 concerns propositional logic and records the roles of subject pronouns and syntactic time markers in Navajo reasoning patterns. Finally, Chapter 7 places human reasoning patterns in the context of general social theory.

This book makes use of previously published material in several places. Excerpts from John Ross's "Gapping and the Order of Constituents," in *Progress in Linguistics,* edited by Manfred Bierwisch and Karl Heidolph, is used with permission of Mouton. Parts of Chapter 2 appeared earlier as James F. Hamill, "Theory in Ethno-Logic," *Symbolic Interaction* 8 (1): 85–102, and much of Chapter 4 was published as Hamill, "Syllogistic Reasoning and Taxonomic Semantics," *The Journal of Anthropological Research* 35 (Winter 1979): 481–94. I would like to acknowledge and thank the publishers of this material for granting their permission to use it.

I also refer in the book to some of the research projects in which I have participated. Several institutions funded that research and I would like to thank them for their support. The University of

Wisconsin-Milwaukee supported the work that I did in Wisconsin. Support for my work on the Navajo Indian Reservation came, at various times, from the College of Arts and Science of Miami University, the Faculty Research Committee of Miami University, and the Wenner-Gren Foundation for Anthropological Research.

Friends and colleagues who contributed significant critical insight to the development of the ideas in this book include George Esber, Georg Vollweiler, Oswald Werner, James Silverberg, Robert Harrison, Alvin Wolfe, Ann Davis, John Johnson, Adolph Greenberg, George Fathauer, and Marvin Loflin. I will always be in their debt. I also wish to acknowledge the help and support I received from the Ojibwa, Mende, Anglo, and Navajo people who were my friends, interpreters, and consultants in the field. Several editors, including John Landsman, Sandra Sebastian, Sandra Manning, and Gerald Meluch gave my manuscripts special care, and they have my gratitude. Special thanks must go to my wife, Lee, who saw to it all. Any remaining errors are my own.

Ethno-Logic

Introduction

About twenty years ago I decided to become an anthropologist. At that time I was in college studying to become an engineer, after having served my country in a war with which I did not agree. I wanted to find out how people could build peace and avoid destruction. I was the product of thirteen years of Catholic education; that experience had trained me to think with some rigor, but had promoted a moral orthodoxy I had come to view as contributing to the world's problems rather than solving them.

Among anthropologists I found a more compelling view: that different ways of life were equal; that no god had endowed anybody with any special standing. I saw how cultural relativism would weaken the excuses used to justify racism, imperialism, and colonialism. Because there were no constraints on the theory of cultural relativism as I was learning it from my professors, I believed that it could not be true as stated. Supposedly any culture I could imagine was a possible human culture, but everything I was learning about people belied that theory. For instance, all peoples organize themselves into families; there are no herds, no gaggles, no pods. In fact, there is nothing but families, all of which fall into a narrow range of variability at that. Cultural relativism, it seemed, could not explain that fact.

I found myself in a dilemma: ethnocentrism was repugnant, but cultural relativism did not hold up well to the facts. Transformational-generative linguistic theory provided a way to pass through the horns of the dilemma. Admittedly, most aspects of the theory do not apply to culture. Its arcane components like "transformational rule" and "deep structure," among others, are clearly inappropriate. On the other hand, the transformational-generative theory constrains variability while placing equal value on all observed variants: there are always some forms that language cannot take, but all languages are equally complex and equally good.

The general theory of language consists of innately endowed

knowledge about language. In transformational theory, the phrase "general theory of language" is synonymous with the phrase "language acquisition device" (LAD). In other words, the general theory of language is the innate knowledge that people bring to the task of learning their language. The LAD explains the ease with which children learn their immensely complex language. Culture is at least as complex as language; children acquire it as easily as they acquire language, and the way cultures vary is similar to the way languages vary. These facts lead me to believe that children bring innate knowledge to the task of learning culture. Here I will draw the same equation that generative linguists draw. I will refer to this innate knowledge of culture as the general theory of culture. The patterns with which people manipulate meanings are a small part of the total scope of the general theory of culture. This book reports some of my research on the relationships between language, culture, and patterned thought. It is my start on a rationalist, Chomskian anthropology.

I begin with the assumption that thinking is one of many cognitive processes. These processes work together to help produce human action and social life. At the same time, what people do feeds back to modify people's thinking patterns. Both for people as individuals and for people as members of social groups—American, Navajo, or any other—patterned thinking is one of the major processes used to create social life.

These assumptions lead me to believe that an understanding of human thinking patterns must lie at the basis of all social theory. All of the things that people make and do are signs of the culture they know. People use their knowledge to draw conclusions, support their beliefs, and interpret new situations. They process knowledge by linking meanings together in patterns that produce new meanings and perhaps new patterns. Some social scientists view these patterns as a black box and are satisfied to correlate "input" with "output." Others, however, may find it more appropriate to view them as integral parts of all social life, of all segments of the social system.

I want to link structure, or patterns, with meaning. The link is not merely that structure expresses meaning, but that structure and meaning interact; they reinforce and modify one another. Patterns that all people share, regardless of their linguistic or cultural heritage, may define humanity to a significant degree, and they emerge from meanings that all people share. Patterns found in only one culture serve to describe that culture and emerge from meanings peculiar to that culture. Thus culture contains logic (i.e., patterned thought) at the particular, descriptive, ethnographic level, which is derived from the universal, explanatory, ethnological level.

Although there is a characteristically human way to think, many animals, and maybe even other living things, also have characteristic ways of thinking. And human thinking has elements in common with all other types of thinking. Nevertheless, it is also clear that human thinking has unique features and unique combinations of features. The way people think is part of the general theory of culture. All people are born with an innate knowledge of logical structure, which they use to produce different logical patterns in different linguistic and cultural settings. The logic found in college textbooks—Western logic—is one example of how people think. Other logical forms evolved outside western European culture; any anthropology of human reasoning must treat these forms as equal to the European forms. Finally, I believe that both universal and culture-specific ways of reasoning are explained most clearly in terms of meaning.

The Contents of Research

Most of the data that I use to support the above ideas are taken from my research. I collected data over a long time in the Mende, Ojibwa, English, and Navajo languages in two separate settings. The first was in Milwaukee, where I participated in a bicultural education project. The second setting was the central Navajo Indian Reservation near Chinle, Arizona.

In Milwaukee I elicited syllogistic information in English, Ojibwa, and Mende from five principal consultants. The five ranged in age from five to nearly seventy years and had from one to seventeen years of Western education. Except for one English speaker, all were bilingual; the Mende speakers were biliterate. The English speaker, a white middle-class male, was five years old when the research began in the early 1970s. The Mende speakers were men in their mid-twenties who were pursuing postgraduate studies at a local university. They had been born in rural Sierra Leone and had been educated in Mende during the first five years of their schooling. The two Ojibwa consultants had less formal education. One, a middle-aged construction worker, had dropped out of school after the eighth grade. The other, an elderly medicine man, had not attended school beyond the third grade. The younger of the two could read and write in English; neither could read or write in Ojibwa. I had regular and frequent contact with all five consultants for over three years in the course of research I conducted on various topics. I interviewed them in locations that were comfortable for them, in homes, taverns, and offices; and I interspersed my ethno-logical interviews with ones related to other research questions.

On the central Navajo Indian Reservation near Chinle, over a ten-year period, I collected all of the propositional data and some of the syllogistic data discussed in this book. Beginning in the mid-1970s, I spent summers on the reservation, conducting research and supervising students in an ethnographic field school. The Navajo syllogistic data were elicited from three consultants, two men and a woman. One man had recently graduated from high school and was bilingual and biliterate in Navajo and English. I collected data from him near his home in the Rough Rock Chapter. (A chapter is a Navajo geopolitical unit similar to a county.) The two other consultants were in their late sixties and lived in the Round Rock area. They were monolingual in Navajo; neither was able to read or write or had any formal education.

I collected formal propositional data from a total of nineteen consultants, ten women and nine men, who ranged in age from their early twenties to their late sixties. These consultants had from zero to fourteen years of formal education, with about six years on the average. Seven spoke only Navajo and twelve were bilingual; five of the latter were biliterate. The propositional research was conducted on the central reservation in the Rough Rock, Round Rock, Many Farms, Chinle, Lukachukai, and Tsaile chapters.

Background Assumptions

A Chomskian anthropology assumes that people create cultural meanings out of innate knowledge; some meanings are panhuman, and others are particular to single cultures. Universal meanings make for universal patterns of reasoning; meaning found in only one language or culture results in a unique logic. For the most part earlier work in ethno-logic did not use meaning to describe human logic but evaluated thinking in Aristotelian terms. Thus thinking patterns were considered significant only if they differed from the western European norm. Too often researchers explained their data by referring to so-called primitive patterns, stating that "primitive" peoples reasoned poorly, if they reasoned at all.

This is problematic because, as I will show later, the data display both universal patterns in human thought and patterns found in only one language and culture. These data demonstrate that no purely formal (that is, meaning-free) concept of logic can describe people's reasoning patterns. When logic is expressed in semantic structures (abstract representations of meanings and relationships between meanings), however, these data can be explained without reference to ad hoc and scientifically empty notions such as "primitive thought."

Because thinking patterns are behind all human action, social theory should include a solid understanding of how people think. Philosophical logic views logic as abstract, not as linked with human activity, in contrast with ethno-logic and the social sciences, which view human thinking as a process that occurs in linguistic, social, and cultural settings. Recently researchers in cognitive science from a variety of disciplines have studied issues in ethno-logic. Unfortunately they have often used the standards of philosophical logic to judge the subjects of their studies. I assume that a firm grasp of how people think can be achieved only through studies that describe thinking patterns from the subject's point of view.

This assumption presents a serious methodological problem because it means that ethno-logical research must find ways to reveal tacit knowledge structures. Ethno-logic, like other areas of study that seek to describe tacit knowledge, can use the mistakes that people make to solve this problem. The fact that people make mistakes shows that they assign meanings to objects and events in their world and compare those meanings to their expectations of the objects and events. Errors can be intentional or unintentional; individuals need not know that something is a mistake in order for the mistake to exist. Furthermore, individual acts can be mistakes in one sense but correct in another. No act or event, in and of itself, can be an error outside its context and the expectations that are tied to it. These expectations emerge from people's beliefs, knowledge, and ideas about their universe. Therefore the analysis of error is a strong methodological tool for uncovering the basic knowledge systems, including reasoning patterns, that make up any culture.

Generative linguists offer a good model for using errors in research. Almost all arguments in generative linguistics rely heavily on the juxtaposition of grammatical strings with ungrammatical strings. By identifying error, linguists expose and describe our knowledge of language. Like language, reasoning patterns are structured and partially generated from underlying rules. That is, some possible examples of both reasoning patterns and language are well formed (reasonable or grammatical), while others are not. Therefore researchers in ethno-logic can apply the structure of inquiry that developed in generative linguistics to the study of reasoning. When research methods generate and consider complete patterns of valid and invalid arguments, it is possible to describe the thinking patterns used by native speakers.

I carried out specific research projects that looked at both syllogistic and propositional reasoning. Syllogisms are classic philosophical logic forms, and their simple structure promotes straightforward methods and easy comparison of languages. In the syllogistic research I sought to describe how consultants respond to syllogistic arguments and avoided stating whether a given response was correct or incorrect in Western terms.

The results of research on the ethno-logic of syllogisms show that people respond to categorical reasoning problems in much the same way all over the world. The response patterns in the four languages I studied, however, differ significantly from the syllogistic reasoning found in Western logic textbooks. The textbook rules that define valid syllogisms cannot account for these findings, but taxonomic, or "kind of," semantics can.

Propositional reasoning combines premises with logical operators such as "and" and "or" to form arguments. I studied the effects of both subject pronouns and syntactic time markers on Navajo propositional arguments. In both studies, the Navajo truth conditions differed from those in Anglo-American patterns. These results can be understood in light of the social and political meanings of acts in the Navajo worldview. Navajo social life stresses order and harmony within a cyclic view of time; Navajo political processes emphasize group consensus. The benefit of using political and social meanings in explaining logical patterns calls into question any view of human reasoning that concentrates strictly on structural factors.

From my research I have developed a view of reasoning that uses meaning to define logical structures. Besides being a part of culture, logic and meaning are interdependent: logic without meaning would be empty, and meaning without a way of processing it would be stagnant. Together logic and meaning are used to produce the new meanings and new patterns of thought that account for the cultural diversity on earth. Behind this diversity, however, are meanings and patterns of thought that all people know. This innate universal knowledge is as fundamentally important to humans as hands or feet or eyes, and it is through this knowledge that we learn our native culture. Because it is the base from which all cultures derive, this knowledge is the general theory of culture.

The general theory of culture must account for both cultural particulars and universals. In the case of my research, the theory must account for the particulars of Navajo and Anglo-English logical patterns and explain equally well why all people err and why all people respond in the same way to certain logical tasks. Therefore the theory must include universals of both meaning and process.

The "kind of" semantic link is only one of the meanings all people share. A basic human logic keyed to semantics makes use of meaning structures in spelling out both logical errors and valid forms. In cases of results such as the propositional findings, the general theory of culture explains the observed differences in logical patterns by pointing to different meanings—by describing the semantic structure of reasoning, which is the part of the general theory of culture that explains the observations made in ethno-logical research.

Meaning, Logic, and Culture   1

People know their own culture. Knowledge is both overt and tacit and includes both matters of fact (theories of the universe, culture) and processes (logic, reasoning). These processes use, generate, and modify facts. Everything that people do or make comes about because they use their knowledge to interact with what is around them. People are able to write books, conduct ceremonies, make pots, or trade ritual goods because they know how to do these things. Thus, an understanding of culture entails an understanding of the knowledge that constitutes culture.

People tend to regard knowledge as something of a catalog of facts, ideas, and beliefs. This viewpoint makes it possible to represent knowledge in the form of easily understood lists, but, unfortunately, lists make it difficult to relate knowledge to issues such as creativity and interpretation. People constantly create and interpret the world around them. For this reason cultural knowledge cannot be reduced to a mere list of things known. Creation and interpretation are processes, but the list is a static device. Knowledge is not a mere roster of things known; rather, like language, it involves the generation of infinite output from finite input. Knowledge is a process of knowing.

Knowledge certainly includes information, but one should not conflate the two. For instance, most of the people whom I interact with every day know something about cars and also distinguish cars from trucks. Yet their knowledge of vehicles cannot alone account for the fact that they distinguish cars from trucks. The explanation is that people make connections between information and sensory inputs; they perceive and create interpretations of the things around them.

It is not useful to separate the information that culture entails, which makes up culture, from any other kind of knowledge. The informational aspect of culture defines much of the familiar world (such-and-such is beautiful; so-and-so is a chief), yet knowledge is dynamic: to use information people also must know how to apply it and how to change it, for instance, how to reinterpret it. In other words, cultural knowledge must include ways to process information (i.e., interpret it, reason with it) and ways by which the information can modify the processes (i.e., new ways to interpret, new reasoning patterns). It must give people the ability to interpret the world around them and to create responses to it.

I assume that these processes take place in a biological context. A logical extension of this idea is that the cultural forms found in most societies around the world have probably emerged from human psychology (D'Andrade 1981:182). These assumptions are an important part of cognitive anthropology and generative linguistics (Chomsky 1974; Fodor 1975). In many ways they unify these fields with cognitive psychology (Dennett 1978), cognitive science (Weizenbaum 1976), and philosophy (P. S. Churchland 1980; P. Churchland 1984). These assumptions are apparent in research seeking to connect mental states with biological states. They also appear in theoretical discussions that delimit the nature of the research problem. This work makes no claims concerning neuropsychology; I have neither the interest in the field nor the knowledge necessary to make such claims. I hope, however, to contribute to our comprehension of the relationship between what people know and how they use what they know.

In western European culture we have a long tradition of intellectual investment in technological analogues to human reason. Clocks, looms, and computers are some of the signposts marking the evolution of our ideas on automata. The most current signpost is artificial intelligence (AI).

The goal of AI research is to develop computer programs that perform some of the intellectual feats that people perform everyday. A well-known example is the diagnosis of disease from a series of symptoms. The basic approach to the problem, the "expert system," tries to encapsulate human knowledge and skill within a set of rules (Waldrop 1987). This approach may result in better computer systems, but it fails to capture what people actually do when they reason. It creates no new knowledge (e.g., it cannot identify a new disease) and no new reasoning patterns (e.g., it cannot develop a new way to connect disease with symptoms).

I am not trying to draw any connection between my work and AI; I am attempting to understand some of the relationships between knowledge, culture, thought, and action. Moreover, I am not trying to build a machine that will mimic those relationships. It will please me if scholars conducting AI research can use my work, but that is not my goal. I hope to make a small contribution to the understanding of how people act—to anthropological theory.

Some theories in the social sciences deny the importance of cultural knowledge, but none, as far as I know, denies its existence. In anthropology, functionalism and cultural materialism are classic examples of theories that ignore what people know. Although both theories acknowledge that people know things and manipulate symbols, in neither theory does knowledge have much relation to the form and content of any culture. Functionalists view culture as a series of institutions, such as the family or the state, that are cultural responses to basic needs. Natives obey, without comprehension, the institutional forces around them (Malinowski 1922:1–25). According to functionalist theories, what people know and how they comprehend the world around them are unimportant. It is the institution whose operation determines daily life. Much the same is true of cultural materialism. In this more current version of functionalism, native knowledge is a mere rationalization of responses to infrastructural forces (Harris 1979:46–76). In other words, anthropologists do not need to understand what natives know in order to understand what natives do.

Determinism

Determinism is the common thread in functionalism and in cultural materialism. Both theories view behavior as the end product of a limited number of social forces, which exist independently of people. Both also explain behavior as a natural consequence of those forces; they claim that the interaction of mechanistic social forces determines what people do.

Because no machine can create, no mechanistic social force can explain the lives that people create for themselves. Social theory cannot and should not attempt to predict what people will do in response to any situation; rather it should try to understand the systems of thought and knowledge that stand behind behavior.

The various aspects of cultural knowledge, including encyclopedic knowledge and the processes through which people use that knowledge, are not separate entities. They do not exist in separate compartments in the mind, but are part of an integrated whole, in which the parts interact with and modify each other. The nature of the parts and the interactions and modifications can be conceived of in many different ways. Piaget et al. (1977) applied development theory to knowledge and defined it as the assimilation of reality into systems of transformations. This view emphasizes the interactions between subject and object. It conceives of knowledge as processes by which objects become subjective and subjects learn about objects (Boyle 1982). Knowledge integrates the individual and the external world;

thus, in many ways, subjects and objects are indistinct from one another (Boyle 1982:298).

Logic, as a cognitive skill, enters into Piagetian development theory with formal operations, which require an abstract model of thought (much like the propositional calculus). Like knowledge, logic is interactive rather than a static, pure, abstract structure. If a child is to develop the ability to perform formal operations, he or she must manipulate the environment physically and mentally. The child must build general patterns of thought from the results of those manipulations (Tomlinson-Keasey 1982:132–48). Formal thought is not merely abstract structure imposed on the world but a complex product of interactions between the mind and the world.

Developmental theories do not have a monopoly on contextualized theories of thought. Early in the twentieth century Vygotsky proposed a theory of higher mental functions such as voluntary attention, remembering, and logical problem solving. He approached these complex psychological functions as cultural and instrumental mechanisms. The higher mental functions are cultural because societies organize tasks that people perform and provide people with the mental and physical tools to master them. Higher mental functions are instrumental in that they mediate between stimuli and behavior; people modify stimuli through processes such as interpretation and use those modifications to act (Luria 1979:38–45). In the Vygotskian approach, reasoning is viewed as a complex social and historical process involving both structure and meaning. Today, Michael Cole and his associates, among others, use this approach to demonstrate the cultural and instrumental features of information processing (Cole, Gay, and Glick 1968), literacy (Scribner and Cole 1981), and syllogistic reasoning (Scribner 1975).

My approach is similar to both Vygotsky's and Piaget's. I define reasoning in more than structural terms, and I regard structure as a feature meaning. In other words, structure and meaning are interdependent. Meaning carries knowledge; people add to their knowledge when new information interacts with previous knowledge through established processes. Likewise, established knowledge modifies processes.

Culture is knowledge, and people gain knowledge through the processes they use to manipulate it. Thus people can acquire culture only from an innate base. I bring a rationalist bias to my work, believing that people are equipped at birth, or before birth, with all of the knowledge they need to master their culture. Furthermore, the cultures that people acquire derive from that innate base.

Culture and language share many important features with respect to rationalist theory. Culture, like language, is extremely complex; thus its acquisition is a major intellectual feat. Because culture resides in the mind and because cognitive capacities are distributed randomly across the human species, all cultures are equally difficult to acquire. Yet children acquire their culture as easily and as rapidly as they acquire their language. They know how to act appropriately in most social situations by the time they are seven or eight years old. They learn these skills in about the same length of time, regardless of their culture and whether or not they receive formal instruction.

This cultural analogue to the language acquisition device underlies much of the recent work in ethnosemantics and sociolinguistics. Ethnosemanticists take a "top down" approach to universals; D'Andrade (1981) assumes explicitly that linguistic and cultural universals are likely to have biological reality. Werner and Schoepfle (1987:96–97) argue that at least some cultural knowledge is transmitted genetically. On the other hand, sociolinguists try to explicate the content of universal phenomena occurring in real conversational settings. These scholars combine aspects of linguistic, social, sociolinguistic, and cultural knowledge in a single construct, namely communicative competence (Baugh and Sherzer 1984; Gumperz and Hymes 1972). They have found that processes such as turn taking, theme development, topic change (Gumperz 1979), alternation, and co-occurrence (Ervin-Tripp 1972) occur universally but express themselves in the form of specific cultural knowledge. Furthermore, people gain communicative competence in the context of cultural relationships that exemplify the cognitive processes underlying human action (Schieffelin 1984).

Processes of thought are a part of all the activity that social theories seek to explain. Therefore, those social theories that do not describe how people think are incomplete. In western European culture we have developed a specialized body of knowledge, called logic, which some claim answers the question How do people think?

Logic, as it has evolved in our culture, concerns consistency within certain defined limits; one such limit is the absence of meaning. That is, logic in Western culture is about the form of reasoning, and logicians avoid connecting logical forms to any content. As a result of this constraint, our view of logic is almost purely formal. Some contemporary logicians claim that logic is only formal and has no relation at all to how people think (Quine 1960). Yet this view considers no real data and thus has only limited utility in social theory.

Ethno-logic, however, is the social science of how people think in the context of what people do, and it does consider real data. Two broad schools of thought in ethno-logic exist today, and they emerged in the early twentieth century. The relativist school contends that reasoning is an artifact of language and culture. Extreme relativists contend that reasoning has no panhuman basis and that validity in one cultural setting means nothing in any other. Because meanings cannot cross the boundaries of language and culture under this extreme view, it eliminates the possibility of research in ethno-logic.

The colonial school contends that all human thought falls under two basic logical modes, the civilized and the primitive. The civilized mode is abstract and hypothetical, and it values consistency. The primitive mode is immediate and concrete and cares little for consistency. This theory, like relativism, holds that reasoning is sensitive to language and culture, but it does little to increase our understanding of human reasoning processes. It merely uses a derogatory or romantic term to label thinking patterns that differ from those of the "civilized" researcher.

Relativist researchers must anchor their ideas in a comparative context before they can give any account of human reasoning processes. Relativistic theories require comparative data that demonstrate conclusively that human thinking patterns have common features across linguistic and cultural boundaries. Likewise, the only way to counter any ethnocentric claim about primitive mentality is to explain cross-cultural variation in neutral terms. Demonstrating common reasoning patterns and explaining cross-cultural variation require descriptions of reasoning grounded in the subjects' point of view. Thus ethnography forms the basis of ethno-logic.

Creativity

Some formulations of experimental theory in social science require that the objects under study be observable (Bloomfield 1926; Harris 1979; Skinner 1953). This condition forces an unfortunate constriction of science, justified only by its poor analogy to the experimental model typical of the physical sciences. Social scientists who insist on this condition believe that the intellectual rigor enjoyed by the physical sciences depends on rigid adherence to a direct observability requirement. Therefore they place a high value on the direct observability of the theoretical entities they postulate.

Science does not concern the ability to literally see phenomena, however. It concerns the ability to understand and to check any understanding against the real world. Scientists need not be able to see what they claim exists; rather, they must be able to imagine the evidence that would lead them to believe that their understanding is wrong. Often, maybe even in most cases, long chains of reasoning connect evidence to ultimate questions; thus it should not be surprising that even physical scientists do not strictly adhere to the observability requirement. They commonly hypothesize the existence of unobservables, such as electrons and quarks, to increase their understanding.

One damaging result of rigid adherence to the observability requirement is that it discourages the consideration of meaning in anthropological research. All examples of reasoning that researchers collect in the field, however, at the most basic level are couched in a matrix of meaning; thus researchers cannot interpret ethno-logical data unless they can interpret the meanings in the data. In addition, if ethno-logic's methods cannot consider meaning, then ethno-logical theory can consider only formal accounts of human thought.

When researchers cannot directly observe the elements that make up a body of study, they must study those elements by observing their effects—through indirect observation. This is as true for the "hard" sciences, such as anthropology and sociology, as it is for the "easy" sciences, such as physics and chemistry. I recognize that my use of "hard" and "easy" turns around the usual classification of the sciences into hard (physics, chemistry) and soft (sociology, anthropology). My classification is a crude measure of the interaction between the elements under study and the researcher: there is not much interaction in the hard sciences, and there is a great deal of interaction in the soft sciences.

Largely for this reason, research in the physical sciences is easier to conduct than social science research. The objects studied by the physical sciences do not change their character radically as a result of being studied, unlike the case with the social sciences. The "objects" of social science research are subjects; because they are people, they create new meanings in response to being researched (Andreski 1972: 18–22). Nevertheless, although human creativity makes life difficult for social scientists, it also provides the key for discovering the structures that underlie human behavior.

Errors occur when creativity is possible; creativity is possible when errors occur, no matter where the mistakes come from. An error is an error only because of the knowledge system that creates it. Almost anyone can think of activities that are wrong in one setting but perfectly appropriate in another. Thus it is not a particular act that is in error; the existence of the error lies in the comparison of the act to a system of knowledge that stands behind and generates the act. Through a comparison of mistakes to nonmistakes, the parameters of the underlying system emerge.

The Aristotelian Paradigm

In some ways the whole idea of ethno-logic is ethnocentric: it applies logic, an artifact of western European culture, to other cultures. In the terms of European scholarly institutions, logic has two distinct parts: truth and validity. Premises can be true or false, and the arrangements of those premises can be valid or invalid (conclusions follow or they do not). Since the time of Aristotle, logic has concerned itself with validity. Both the distinction between truth and validity and the selection of validity as the core of logic are cultural choices. They reflect the values of the society that made the choices more accurately than they reflect the truth about the nature of reasoning.

Nevertheless, researchers must start somewhere; typically they start where they are. Anthropology, sociology, and psychology have made significant contributions to our knowledge of how people think, albeit they have emerged from western European culture and therefore proceed from western European values. In ethno-logic the starting point is the Aristotelian point of view.

Like other fields of interest in anthropology, ethno-logic uses ethnographic information to test its ideas. Either implicitly or explicitly, ethnography always compares the subject culture with the audience culture. The question is not whether ethno-logic starts from a culturally biased base but how to interpret that base. Researchers can take the assumptions of philosophical logic as either the norm for all logical systems or the folk logic of their own society.

To take Western logic as the norm for all logical systems clearly begs the question. It cannot lead to significant insights about how people think because observations that do not compare well with a norm, no matter what the norm, are marked—they may be overvalued or undervalued. Thus when ethno-logicians start with Western logic as the norm, they often conclude that non-Western people are logically inferior to Westerners.

A more productive approach is to assume that the Aristotelian view, and the philosophical logics that have developed from it, make up western Europe's folk logic. Thus when researchers compare another logic to Western logic, they are not comparing it to a norm but to another folk system. The theoretical challenge in ethno-logic is to explain the similarities between folk logics and reconcile the differences between them. To meet this challenge ethno-logicians must collect data that expose those similarities and differences.

Many researchers have chosen syllogisms as the basis for these comparative data. Syllogisms are three-statement arguments consisting of a major premise, a minor premise, and a conclusion. Each statement posits a class-inclusion relationship between the subject and the predicate. Syllogisms have the advantage of being simple and straightforward. They are also very well described, since Western academic logic concentrated on syllogisms from the time of Aristotle's original formulation of them until the early twentieth century. As a result, the structural factors leading to valid syllogistic conclusions are well known and easy to use.

Since the early writings of Lévy-Bruhl in 1926, there have always been some social scientists who maintained a distinction between civilized and primitive thought. At first impression this distinction has little to recommend it. It does not explain how or why people think; it merely labels thinking patterns according to how they compare with the western European norm. On the other hand, the distinction between logical and mystical thought describes some important features of human thought: humans do indeed think mystically, and they do think logically. Lévy-Bruhl, however, rejected the notion that people think either mystically or logically depending on whether they live in civilized or primitive cultures. Rather, he believed that all people think both mystically and logically. To Lévy-Bruhl, the scientist thinks as mystically as the Navajo hand-trembler, and the Navajo thinks as logically as the scientist. Unfortunately, this part of Lévy-Bruhl's thought has gone unnoticed in some of the recent reformulations of his theory.

Given the fact that humans reason, ethno-logicians face two tasks. They must determine what patterns of thought vary with language and culture, and they must propose theories to explain why they do. Logical patterns are both general and selective: they are general in the sense that they apply to any topic of discussion; they are selective in the sense that some structures of discourse are invalid, that is, they do not allow a conclusion. The syllogism is a logical pattern found in every language and culture researched thus far. Therefore, ethno-logical theory must explain why consultants always respond to syllogism tests in the same way. It should also explain why consultants draw syllogistic conclusions and why they sometimes draw them in the same patterns regardless of language or culture. Equally, the theory must explain why some logical patterns are found only in a particular language and culture. To identify logical patterns, researchers often study propositional reasoning.

Russell's Revolution

Logicians studied syllogisms until the publication, in 1910, of *Principia Mathematica,* in which Whitehead and Russell set out to prove that mathematics is a part of logic. After *Principia,* the syllogism had to compete with a new kind of logic. To accomplish their goal Whitehead and Russell had to abandon syllogisms because it is impossible to derive a number from them. They developed a logic that, unlike the syllogism, does not depend on class-inclusion relationships. Instead, the newer logic employs premises and operators. The premises must be propositions (statements that are either true or false), hence the name of this logic: the propositional calculus.

The propositional calculus is based on the two primitive operators "and" and "not," which are defined by truth tables. For example, if any proposition "P" is true, then "not P" is false. From this base it is possible to derive other operators—"or," "if . . . then," and "if and only if"—as well as fundamental mathematical statements ($1 + 1 = 2$, for example). The impact of Whitehead and Russell's work on our culture cannot be overstated. It forms the theoretical basis of the digitalized world we are creating today.

Ethno-logicians find both syllogisms and the propositional calculus attractive. The study of syllogisms can suggest the effects of culture on reasoning because true class-inclusion relationships vary with culture. The effect of language on thought patterns is easily studied through research using the propositional calculus; for example, such research has revealed that "and" and "not" are found in the syntax of all languages (Greenberg 1963). Using the propositional calculus, ethno-logicians can collect data that reveal the logic behind propositional arguments and can compare logics across linguistic boundaries.

The methods used to collect these data are much like those used to collect syllogistic data. In both cases consultants respond to a set of arguments; they judge the arguments to be either valid (a conclusion follows) or invalid (a conclusion does not follow). If the set contains all possible argument structures, then the distribution of valid arguments can reveal the data's underlying logic. Each premise must be either true or false to a consultant and must be given in the consultant's native language.

Quine (1960:57–58) outlined a method for studying propositional logics that serves as the basis for most recent research. In this method the researcher first collects the raw material in the consultant's native language and uses this material to construct the argument set. The arguments include the conjoiners used to connect each premise with another and the premises themselves. Next, the researcher constructs the argument set so that all combinations of true and false premises appear with each conjoiner. The researcher then gives each argument in the set to the consultants and notes their judgments as to their validity.

This is a laborious, time-consuming process that quickly exhausts the patience of even the most tolerant consultant. Even so, the result can be an accurate description of the structure, or syntax, of propositional reasoning in the consultant's language and culture. This method, in all of its varieties, is an empirical copy of propositional logic as found in textbooks; thus the results automatically are comparable to that logic. Unfortunately, though, it does not provide any information on how people use reason in everyday life.

The textbook version of propositional logic is simple, straightforward, and powerful, but the empirical version studied by ethnologicians is much more complex. The textbook logic preserves truth in a simple manner (McKenna 1986). It might hold, for instance, that the statement "A and B" is true only when both "B" and "A" are true. If either is false, or if both are false, then the entire statement is false. The textbook logic says nothing at all about the actual truth of "A" or "B"; it merely defines the truth of the whole conjunct for all the possible truth conditions of the propositions. In contrast, the empirical logics seem to preserve not only truth but also other elements that are clearly cultural. Political values and ideas about the nature of time are present in the empirical logics. These logics cannot be described as merely true or false; their descriptions also must include meanings that vary with culture.

Using political, temporal, or other meaning structures to describe logical patterns makes it appear as if people in different cultures use different logics. Yet if ethno-logical theory merely described the variations found in the data, it would have little to recommend it. Ethno-logical theory should explain both syllogistic and propositional data; it must explain why conclusions follow from both syllogistic and propositional arguments. It also must explain how conclusions follow, why syllogisms seem to be universal, and why propositional arguments seem to be culture-sensitive.

The Anthropology of Logic

Logical patterns are part of people's knowledge about their culture; these patterns are part of all human action and can set one culture apart from another. In philosophical logic they are abstract and are not linked to any human activity. In ethno-logic they are part of what people do when they talk and interact with one another. From this point of view, reasoning is a process that occurs in linguistic, social, and cultural settings.

Recently, anthropologists, developmental psychologists, and

other scholars working under the rubric of cognitive science have studied issues in ethno-logic. Unfortunately, however, much of their work uses philosophical logic as the norm by which to judge subjects' responses. Certainly philosophical logic is important to research in ethno-logic; it is a reliable guide to the development of research techniques that allow researchers to approach important issues. Yet an understanding of how people think can come only from studies that describe thinking patterns from the consultants' point of view. Philosophical logic's value is in helping to produce methods that allow both universal and culture-specific patterns of reasoning to be identified. Valid arguments are explained by reference to the patterns of meaning that people use to make their cases.

The problem with using meaning to explain and describe reasoning patterns is that meanings are notoriously unobservable. Therefore ethno-logicians need some principled means of reaching the meanings that stand behind what they see. The study of errors or mistakes provides that means. An error or mistake is a discontinuity between what is known and what occurs, when the meaning of a particular event runs contrary to the general system of knowledge or values in the context of the event. A rock cannot make a mistake because it has no knowledge and thus cannot assign meaning. The reverse, of course, is true of people. The fact that people call some events mistakes suggests that they assign meanings to events, which they compare to their expectations about the events. Therefore, the study of error is a strong methodological tool for uncovering those basic knowledge systems which make up culture.

Generative linguistics has used ungrammatical sentences to expose the linguistic processes, both universal and particular, that make up a native speaker's knowledge of language. Ethno-logic uses a similar method because a knowledge system, to be logical, must define validity, meaning that under a logic system, some argument structures must fail to lead to conclusions. Ethno-logic can define the logical systems used by native speakers only when both correct and incorrect arguments are studied.

The syllogism lends itself to ethno-logical research because its logic is well known; its valid and invalid forms have been described thoroughly. In addition, as stated earlier, its structure makes for straightforward methods and easy comparison of languages. To avoid the ethnocentrism of using Western logic as a norm, researchers should use the syllogism to simply describe logical patterns. They should not concern themselves with whether the patterns are correct or incorrect in Western terms.

The first step in my syllogistic research was to elicit four sentence frames glossed as "All A is B," "No A is B," "Some A is B," and "Some A is not B." Next I filled the variables (the As and the Bs) to produce a set of premises that the consultants agreed were true. I found that I could generate all sixty-four possible syllogisms from a set of twenty-one premises. After the consultants agreed that all sentences were true, they responded to each of the syllogisms with whatever conclusions they wished.

In the past I found it convenient to use words in a "folk taxonomy" to fill the frames. These words are related to one another with "kind of" semantics ("S is a kind of R"). Because the syllogism is a form of class-inclusion logic, a proper cross-cultural test of syllogistic reasoning must consider class-inclusion meaning systems. When I began this research, anthropologists considered folk taxonomies to be universal semantic domains, but since that time a more sensible view has emerged. Many anthropologists now regard folk taxonomies as artifacts of method: we collect them, and so we find them, but they do not fully represent how people conceptualize their world (Kay 1975:151–54).

The more current view is that words may be connected to other words in many ways. Nevertheless, the "kind of" semantic relationship is important because we find it in all languages (Casagrande and Hale 1967; Spradley 1981; Werner and Schoepfle 1987; Werner and Topper 1976). Thus reseachers are led to construct classifications, such as folk taxonomies, that do not necessarily represent how people actually understand their world. In any case, my syllogism research did not aim to discover how people view their world and organize its material; rather, it sought to understand how people used "kind of" semantics in patterned thought.

The consultants' responses to the syllogism tests display an amazing consistency. The consultants never drew invalid conclusions (invalid in Western terms), and in some cases they rejected valid conclusions (valid according to logic textbooks). All valid conclusions that were rejected were particular statements for which the corresponding universal statement was true (e.g. "Some A is B" where "All A is B" is true). Since the philosophical rules that define validity for syllogisms cannot account for these findings, they cannot form the basis of ethno-logical theory.

In addition to this syllogistic research, I conducted propositional reasoning studies that recorded the role of subject pronouns and syntactic time markers in Navajo propositional logic. The methods used in both of these studies were derived from Quine's outline; they required native speakers of Navajo to judge the validity of arguments arranged in a paradigm. Each study found logical patterns in Navajo that did not occur in English. In addition, both pronouns and time played a role in limiting the validity of Navajo arguments. The Navajo worldview can explain these results: differences in meaning account for the logical differences found between English and Navajo propositional arguments.

To sum up this chapter, any general theory of culture must account for both universal and particular culture. It should explain not only universal error and common responses to syllogism tests, but also particular logical patterns found in only one culture. A good theory, however, cannot merely enumerate the universals and particulars. It must explain them by proposing principles from which both universals and particulars follow. Therefore the theory must include universals of both meaning and process.

The "kind of" semantic link is one of the meanings that all people share. A human logic, keyed to meaning structures in arguments, makes use of that link to spell out both logical errors and valid syllogisms. Where logical patterns differ from one culture to another, different cultural meanings, such as different concepts of time or different political values, can explain the variance. Because the material of culture is knowledge that is encoded in meaning, the semantic structure of arguments explains the observations made in ethnological research.

The Ethnographic Basis of Ethno-Logic   2

Some sociologists and anthropologists argue that people act in response to social forces; how people think is considered inconsequential. In sociology the social forces are historical, according to conflict theorists, and institutional, according to structural functionalists. In anthropology, cultural materialists contend that cultural form is determined by its infrastructural base. In this theory, reasoning belongs to the superstructural level of culture along with worldviews, values, and ideology (but not anthropological understanding because that is the result of "scientific" observation). The superstructure is said to contribute little to anthropological understanding because it contains arbitrary cognitive concoctions that people use to justify their structural responses to infrastructural constraints (Harris 1979:265–86).

Harris may be fundamentally correct. People may react to their world in ways that fit some of the distinctions represented by "infrastructure," "structure," and "superstructure." Such reactions would speak more to the workings of the human mind than to the objective "etic" world. A similar analysis could be made in regard to conflict theory and structural functionalism. Therefore, any body of social theory would be refined and strengthened by a firm understanding of the thought processes that underlie individual and group action.

Humans are not automata subject to the caprices of social forces outside themselves. They participate actively in their lives by making decisions and solving problems, using the cognitive tools at their disposal. These tools include a detailed knowledge of their world, their values, and their emotional reactions to situations. These social tools are obvious and are open to social theorists for study. In and of themselves, however, knowledge, values, and feelings are inadequate to explain social life because they are subject to processing in every human activity.

People manipulate their knowledge, values, and feelings to negotiate a common reality with others. To do so they employ thought-processing mechanisms (which are really logics) that use knowledge, values, and feelings. Because logic has cultural aspects, an understanding of social life requires an understanding of how people think in their own cultural context. Ethno-logic is the study of these thought processes and how they are affected by language and culture.

Two Kinds of Logic

Lévi-Strauss (1966:35) defined logic as the "establishment of necessary connections." His elegant statement captures the essence of human reasoning. "Establishment" implies a process in which multiple components may interact; these components are premises, rules for combining premises, and cultural values. "Necessary" tells us that the process is well defined and that it is governed by rules that eliminate some results while allowing others. "Connections" refers to the goal of the reasoning process. As anthropologists we can approach reasoning as an empirical fact, as something human beings do. We can try to develop theories that account for observed instances of reasoning ("ethno-logic"). On the other hand, we can view logic as an abstract process by itself. In this view, logical rules are much like gravity or electromagnetic force; they are abstract and independent of any user. We call these rules "laws of consistency." This is the logic of textbooks.

Scholars who investigate issues in textbook logic begin with a set of primitive elements, rules for combining those elements, and criteria for judging the results of the combinations. The elements can be terms, propositions, or numbers. The rules can take the form of explicit statements, such as "No argument can contain only negative premises," or can be definitions, such as truth tables. Statements like "No thing can be both A and not A in the same sense at the same time" and "All things are either A or not A" make up the criteria by which one may judge the consistency in textbook logics such as mathematics and computer programming.

The goal of textbook logic is the development of internally consistent computational systems. One can work with existing primitives and rules to demonstrate that new statements are true within the system. This process is much like the exercises that high school students do in plane geometry when they prove, for instance, that the shortest distance between two parallel lines is represented by a line perpendicular to the lines. One also may propose new elements or combinatorial rules (or both) and attempt to prove that the new system is consistent. That is, one may propose a new logic.

This characterization of textbook logic is necessarily brief and simplistic, but it captures an essential point about how logicians view logic and its relationship to thinking. Even the most extreme logical formalists agree that logic is expressed through language. For instance, Quine (1986:95–102) presents logic as the product of truth and grammar. At the same time, he claims that logic is empirically real and emerges in the scientific enterprise. Hintikka (1985) also relates language and logic in the context of science; he rejects philosophies of science that view theories as statements or as models for a question/answer paradigm. Instead he sees theories as questions that scientists ask of nature, and he uses that linguistic structure to represent the logic of scientific discovery.

No one should equate Quine with Hintikka, but both scholars regard logic as something independent of people. In their view, our scientific understanding of the empirical world confirms the existence of logic. Yet because logic is independent of what people do, it cannot be discovered through empirical research.

Obviously, textbook logic focuses on the system and not on human reasoning. If textbook logic is able to teach us about human reasoning, it is because logicians are human, a fact that makes their results examples of human reasoning. Unfortunately, if one wants to know how all humans reason, the examples that come from textbook logic have limited applicability. If we observe people reasoning in natural contexts, we will almost never hear any of them using or citing the theorems of textbook logic.

Textbook logic tells us little about how human beings actually reason outside the narrow realms of analytic philosophy or mathematics. This conclusion is neither profound nor new; over twenty years ago Jean-Blaise Grize (1967) suggested that systems of logic should assume psychological and social perspectives. Since that time he has developed his ideas in terms of cognitive functions (Piaget et al. 1977) and contradictions in discourse (Grize 1979). Grize is a developmental psychologist who has worked almost exclusively in western European cultural settings. His research emphasizes the areas in which textbook logic can lead social scientists astray.

Reasoning, at least on the surface, has a cultural component. Social scientists err because they have been inculcated with a view of logic as an abstract system rather than a human activity. Social scientists tend to believe that reasoning is reasoning—that human behavior either stands up to the cold light of logical criticism, or it does not.

This view presents two problems. First, it permits social theories that do not consider social and cultural variability in reasoning patterns. Structural functionalism and conflict theory are only two cases in point. Yet if reasoning patterns conform to the logician's view, they apply equally to all people and thus need not be a part of social theories. Although all the specific patterns of thought found in any culture are derived from some underlying human pattern, they still may vary significantly from culture to culture. Human reasoning patterns do vary with culture, and theories that ignore this fact lose their explanatory power.

The second problem arises for social scientists who recognize that logic, or reasoning, varies with culture. These scholars must deal with an apparent contradiction: the logicians tell them that logic is a natural law, but their research tells them that the human reasoning they observe does not conform to this law. All too often, ethnologicians resolve this contradiction by saying that the logic they observed is wrong, that the people in question are primitive, and that western European societies "know better." This explanation cannot add to our knowledge or understanding. Social scientists must take non-Western natives seriously and recognize that, like Western natives, they are actors in social life.

Whereas textbook logic studies consistency within systems, ethno-logic studies actual human reasoning in its linguistic, social, and cultural context. In order to describe cultures, anthropologists use participant observation, which, in its modern form, combines observations with interviews to produce ethnographies. The more accurately an ethnography reflects the natives' points of view, the better it is.

Ethno-logic is the ethnographic study of human reasoning. Ethno-logical study concerns the process of human thought and attempts to describe the factors that constitute it. Often the systems developed in textbook logic provide the starting point for data collection; therefore studies of syllogisms or of mathematical reasoning among aliterate people are common in the ethno-logical literature. Ethno-logic, however, is not concerned with consistency but instead seeks to explain ethnographic observations.

Studies in ethno-logic emphasize either comparison or description. A comparative study examines intrinsic properties of the study's subjects to determine whether those properties have any effect on the logical systems employed by the subjects. Investigations comparing children to adults, schooled peoples to unschooled ones, literate populations to nonliterate ones, or people in one social class to those in another can easily be found in the ethno-logical literature. Typically, comparative studies measure the subjects' performance on a standardized test. Appropriate groups of subjects take the test, and their responses then are compared. This method is particularly popular in developmental psychological research, in which scholars often apply their background in psychometric testing. Perhaps because of these common testing techniques, comparative studies in ethno-logic are relatively weak in the area of cross-cultural research. They concentrate on subjects who speak Indo-European languages and come from western European cultural backgrounds.

Descriptive studies in ethno-logic do not concern themselves with the connections between social groups and with differences in reasoning patterns but concentrate on in-depth descriptions of reasoning in a particular cultural context. Differences between subjects are not important here; indeed, the more homogeneous the subjects of a particular study are, the better. These studies have an ethnographic emphasis and are common in the anthropological literature. Often, as is the case in much ethnography, descriptive ethno-logic seems to argue to the ethnographer's preexisting biases; ethnographers try to demonstrate that logic is an artifact of culture. Other ethnographers want us to believe that logical reasoning has no fundamental cultural component.

Historical Background

The recent ethno-logical work in anthropology, psychology, and cognitive science does not represent ethno-logic's beginning. Almost from the outset of social science, there were scholars who recognized the importance of finding out how people think. Both Lévy-Bruhl (1926) and Whorf (1964) made early contributions, demonstrating that comparative and descriptive studies were present in some of the earliest ethno-logical research.

Lévy-Bruhl is known for his early work, *How Natives Think,* in which he proposed that a "prelogical mentality" was characteristic of primitive people. Western European thought was rational and discursive, and it required intricate categories, concepts, and abstract terms (Lévy-Bruhl 1926:105). On the other hand, the primitive, prelogical mentality was "little given to analysis," "essentially synthetic," "impervious to experience," and "insensible to contradiction" (Lévy-Bruhl 1926:107–8).

Lévy-Bruhl did not conceive of the prelogical mentality as an inferior, or even as a prior, form of western European logic, but simply saw it as fundamentally different from Western thought. It cared little to avoid incongruity and obeyed instead the "law of participation" (Lévy-Bruhl 1926:78). Thus a Bororo man could be both man and parakeet at the same time because men and parakeets participate in the same collective representation (Lévy-Bruhl 1926:69–104).

In this early work Lévy-Bruhl saw the law of participation and the law of contradiction as parallel modes of cognition. Participation was manifest in primitive societies; contradiction, in civilized societies. Lévy-Bruhl's later work qualified this idea to such an extent that participation was no longer regarded as a "law" and "prelogical mentality" had been supplanted. By the late 1930s Lévy-Bruhl (1975:1–19) conceived of the prelogical as a consequence of the mystical. He viewed participation as a datum, not as a relationship. He also reformulated his views on the relationship between mysticism, logic, and social group: "there is not a primitive mentality distinguishable from the other by *two* characteristics which are peculiar to it (mystical and prelogical). There is a mystical mentality which is more marked and more easily observed among "primitive peoples" than our own societies, but it is present in every human mind" (101). Lévy-Bruhl did not say that primitives think like European children—that idea was to come with more contemporary researchers—but his early work did lay the foundation for comparative ethno-logic. Unfortunately, scholars have ignored his later thinking, which may be far more interesting, in favor of his earlier ideas, which are more comforting to the ethnocentric Western mind.

Whorf had little interest in comparing Western thought patterns to primitive ones at any level. His goal was to describe logical patterns in particular languages in order to expose the fallacies in certain common ideas about human reasoning. In his most famous examples, which came from studies on the Hopi, he attempted to demonstrate that the pattern of Hopi thinking derived from Hopi grammatical categories. He concentrated on syntactic time markers in the Hopi sentence because they are not describable in terms of Indo-European categories. He wished to expose as false the idea that all humans operate from a common logical base. To Whorf, the idea that language is a tool for expressing some underlying natural logic contained two fallacies. One fallacy confused agreement on subject matter with agreement on thought processes; the other assumed that language merely expressed, rather than created, thought.

Whorf saw logic as an artifact of language. Therefore he believed that reasoning patterns derived from the grammar of the native language. Where languages are similar, similar reasoning patterns emerge; where they are different, different reasoning patterns are apparent (Whorf 1964). Whorf's point was not that Hopi logic was better or worse than European logic or that the two patterns both fell on some universal continuum. Rather he wanted to show that Hopi logic was different from European logic as demonstrated by differences in the Hopi and English languages. To make that point, he needed only to describe the logic he found.

Whorf's hypotheses encountered severe criticism in the 1950s and 1960s. Scholars questioned his analysis of Hopi syntax and performed tests of his hypothesis using restricted sets of words, such as color terms. They found little difference in perception between speakers of very different languages. As Kay and Kempton (1984) pointed out, much of this critical research assumed that the Whorfian hypothesis claimed that the "semantic systems of different languages vary without constraint." This is a serious misreading, however; there is good reason to believe that Whorf viewed relativity and linguistic determinism in a restricted sense. Scholars now are reformulating Whorf's ideas to reflect a modified relativity that operates on linguistic, cultural, and individual levels. Silverstein (1979) views the hypothesis in terms of the performative aspects of language, and he presents Whorf as a precursor to Austin. Friedrich (1986) criticizes Whorf for his overemphasis on structure and reformulates Whorfian linguistic relativity in poetic terms to include individual, aesthetic, and imaginative forces in the shaping of thought.

Both Whorf's and Lévy-Bruhl's ideas have been corrupted by simplistic interpretations that distorted many of their most significant insights. Each of those interpretations made a strong connection between thought processes and culture, a connection that neither Whorf nor Lévy-Bruhl made. Lévy-Bruhl, as interpreted, allowed two kinds of logic: an abstract, hypothetical western European pattern and a concrete, childlike primitive pattern. In this colonial model, the civilized (European) patterns are superior and overlie the primitive patterns.

Whereas colonialists allow for only two logics, Whorf, according to the extreme relativist interpretation, allows for as many logics as there are grammars. From Whorf's point of view, western European logic is not superior to or inferior to Hopi logic; it is merely different. It is one of an infinite number of possible logics, each of which has equal status. Today few if any ethno-logicians use this extreme relativist model other than to serve as a straw man because it contains an important flaw: if it were true, ethno-logic would not be possible. The only way in which we can study Hopi logic, or the logic in any culture other than our own, is through universals of thought that apply to all humans. Unfortunately, based on this realization, some scholars have concluded that relativism is dead and have proposed colonial theories to fill the void.

Ethno-Logic Today

Most contemporary ethno-logic is based on Vygotskian psychology or anthropology. A. R. Luria and Michael Cole approach ethno-logic from the psychological perspective; Edwin Hutchins (1980) and C. R. Hallpike (1979), from the viewpoint of anthropology. All four scholars have researched human reasoning outside their home cultural traditions. Cole, Luria, and Hallpike, however, support the colonial view to some degree, whereas Hutchins does not.

Hallpike is a British anthropologist; his field experience includes work among the Konso of Ethiopia (1972) and the Tauade of Papua, New Guinea (1977). Luria's contributions to ethno-logic began in the early 1930s, when he and Vygotsky developed a research program to study intellectual functions in a traditional society (Luria 1979:55–80). Vygotsky's works became known outside the Soviet Union when Michael Cole introduced them in the 1970s. Cole's interests cover a wide range of cognitive processes including memory (Scribner and Cole 1972), classification (Ciborowski and Cole 1973), and learning (Ciborowski and Cole 1972), as well as reasoning (Cole et al. 1971; Cole and Scribner 1974). Since Cole's work concerns the interactions between cognitive processes and culture, it therefore involves a notable cross-cultural component no matter what the subject. Edwin Hutchins's (1980) work on the logic of land tenure cases provides a thorough analysis of culture and thought among Trobriand islanders in Melanesia.

Luria, Cole, and Hallpike couch their ideas about human logic in different terms, but their ideas contain similar features. Luria (1971:271–72) believes that "the operation of reaching a logical conclusion from the syllogism is certainly not of a universal character"; instead, a particular social and historical development produces logical thought. He conceives of two levels of historic development: a simple level, in which "the role of immediate practice dominates," and a more complex level, characterized by concept formation, logical conclusions, and reasoning. Although this scheme is not exactly like Lévy-Bruhl's early idea of prelogical mentality, it is similar in structure, if not in values. Luria envisions two levels of thinkers based on social-group membership. The concrete, practical, everyday thinkers belong to tribal and village cultures, whereas the abstract, conceptual, hypothetical thinkers are members of western European state-level cultures. To Luria the process of logical thinking is a product of Western culture.

In addition to introducing Luria's work and ideas, Michael Cole has researched thought processes in cultures outside western European traditions. He has worked among Mexican peasants (Cole 1973) and Mayan Indians (Sharp, Cole, and Lave 1978), but West Africa was the setting for his most complete and significant work. There he conducted research among the Kpelle (Cole et al. 1971) and the Vai (Scribner and Cole 1978).

In all of his work Cole relies heavily on methods common in experimental psychological research, which requires explicit hypotheses and tests. These methods provide reliable and reproducible results, but they are also limiting. Because the psychometric procedures require researchers to use a hypothesis-testing mode of inquiry, they necessarily define the world for the respondent. Therefore Cole's methods often encourage the development of a colonial model of human reasoning; he relies naively on methods developed in, and appropriate only for, western European subjects. Nonetheless, he must be commended for his thoughtful adaptations of this methodology and for his careful conclusions. Even though his methods impose Western modes on non-Western contexts, he always applies them in native semantic fields. Furthermore, he typically refuses to conclude that the people he studies are deficient thinkers, although his findings have led some scholars (such as Hallpike) to make that conclusion.

Hallpike (1979:32–36) couches his ideas in Piagetian terms. He contends that primitive people (i.e., people who are not members of Western societies) think at the preoperative level of development. In support of his case, Hallpike uses a wide variety of ethnographic literature, including his own studies of the Konso and the Tauade. Interestingly, both Cole's and Luria's works occupy a key position in Hallpike's analysis; without them his return to colonialism carries little weight.

Hutchins, in contrast, stays very close to ethnographic ideals in his explication of Trobriand reasoning and brings a processual view to ethnography. He regards culture not as a set of true statements about the world but as the knowledge of how to make true statements. Hutchins recognizes that much of that knowledge is transparent to people; nonetheless, they have it and use it. The knowledge about how to reason is perhaps the most transparent.

Hutchins approaches the study of Trobriand reasoning patterns by examining legal disputes over land tenure. He demonstrates that the Trobriand people rely on valid inferences in these disputes, and he shows that they are as capable as any other social group of making sound logical arguments. Hutchins's treatment of inferences that appear to contain fallacies according to textbook logic demonstrates the proper ethnographic treatment of this sort of data. He does not simply label these arguments as mistakes and discuss the natives' seeming lack of ability to deal with abstract thought, but instead accepts the data—and the respondents—as they are. Hutchins uses these data to build an understanding of Trobriand reasoning patterns and the Trobriand rules that govern them. He uses the "mistakes" as epistemological windows (Werner and Schoepfle 1987:57–69) to reveal the knowledge system that underlies Trobriand land tenure.

Basic Human Logic

Cole, Luria, and Hallpike have one thing in common: they violate a fundamental principle of ethnography. In certain cases each labels the consultants' responses as mistakes because they do not conform to Western values. If theory is to truly account for data, however, anthropologists cannot label any observation a mistake without referring to the cultural knowledge that makes it a possible mistake. It is a violation of sound ethnographic procedure to label some of the consultants' behavior as errors simply because they do not agree with the researcher's expectations, as Cole, Luria, and Hallpike do. This sort of labeling necessarily leads to ethnocentric conclusions such as "Primitive thought is preoperatory" or "concrete" and does nothing to add to our understanding of how humans actually think.

Hallpike, as a well-trained anthropologist with extensive field experience, should have avoided this type of conclusion and should have been aware of the dangers of applying western European values and norms to non-Western cultures. Cole's understanding of the interaction of culture is much more sophisticated than Hallpike's. He has publicly challenged anthropologists to contribute to the ethno-logical literature (Cole and Scribner 1975) and has proposed a Vygotskian reintegration of psychology and anthropology (Cole 1985).

Although Hallpike strengthens his arguments by drawing on Cole's and Luria's data, he uses much of his own ethnographic data to make his case. When he discusses his own data, he often labels the subjects' behavior as logically deficient. For example, Hallpike criticizes a speech by a Konso chief for its "compressed style," its lack of "logical order," and its failure to develop a theme (Hallpike 1979:113–14). He gives no indication that he attempted to discover whether the speaker intended any logical order in the speech. His most serious violation of ethnographic methods was to ignore completely the listeners' evaluations of the performance. Ethnography offers clear, rigorous methods for discerning the natives' view of the underlying logic; Hallpike disregarded these methods and the natives' view and applied his own values to judge the Konso.

If the Konso were not abstract enough for Hallpike's taste, and thus were illogical, then the Tauade were too abstract. Hallpike draws the distinction between a logical operatory class, all of whose members have at least one thing in common, and a complexive category, which is preoperatory and is "inherently linked with concrete imagery." As an example of a complexive category he points to the Tauade term *ago* and its syntactic derivatives. This term applies to stone, culture heroes, animals, plants, and immortality. He concludes that "there is no single characteristic common to all" of these things. Thus *ago* is a complexive category and not a class (Hallpike 1979:183–86). Yet the word is clearly abstract, not concrete; furthermore, it has wide application to Tauade life. Thus to use the semantics of *ago* to demonstrate preoperatory thought for the Tauade misses the point. The semantics of *ago* do show that the Tauade use meaning that they assign and attributes to things, but they do not address the structure of how the Tauade use meaning. One can conclude that the semantics of *ago* show something about that structure only by making assumptions about what the structure should look like before the data are analyzed.

Fortunately, these methodological errors need not prevent us from making headway in understanding human reasoning. Other competent scientists, including Cole and Luria, have collected and reported explicit information on how people respond to logical problems (logical in the European sense). Because of the wide range of peoples and languages studied, we can use these data to develop new programs of study and thoughtful, powerful theories about how people think, which should provide ethno-logic with new insights.

Luria studied Uzbekhi peasants in the 1930s. His work was originally published in the Soviet Union, but in the early 1970s Michael Cole translated it into English. Luria collected two kinds of data. In one part of his study, he asked respondents to draw a conclusion from syllogisms. These syllogisms dealt with subjects that were either familiar or unfamiliar to the respondent. In the other part of his study, he collected data that were responses to sorting problems. Luria presented the respondents with groups of four picture cards. Three of the cards pictured objects that "were members of well-defined categories"; the "fourth object clearly did not belong to that category" (Luria 1971:267). Luria asked the respondents to select the one card that did not fit with the other three. Obviously, the syllogistic data interest us because they represent instances in which consultants draw conclusions from premises. The sorting test data are also useful because syllogistic logic is categorical logic.

In the category tests Luria defined the world for the respondents. He started with the assumption that three of the pictures in the sorting test represented members of a well-defined category and that the fourth did not belong to that group. His ethnographic error lies in the way in which he expressed the test results: if respondents did not meet his expectations by sorting out the item Luria thought did not belong, he judged their choice to be wrong. His goal was not to describe the world from the consultants' point of view but to find out how well their view fit his own (his view, of course, was "correct"). In light of his assumptions, Luria's conclusions make sense. If one takes a more ethnographic view, however, a completely different conclusion emerges.

The cards that Luria discusses in greatest depth pictured a saw, an axe, a shovel, and a piece of wood. One group of consultants performed as Luria expected; they sorted out the piece of wood from the other three, which he labeled tools. Another group of consultants singled out the shovel as inappropriate. These consultants had no experience with Western education, and they refused to group together the saw, the axe, and the shovel even when prompted with the Uzbekhi word *asbob* (glossed "tool"). They argued that the saw and the axe were necessary to make the piece of wood useful and that the shovel was irrelevant to the other three.

Luria then told his consultants that "one man said that the ax, the saw and the shovel had to be placed together because they are similar to each other; that it is possible to name them with one word; and that the log was not a tool and therefore did not belong" (Luria 1971:268). Yet even after this intense training, the subjects refused to sort out the log, saying "'No, that man was not correct, he does not know his business, he is a fool. Look, the saw and the ax, what could you do with them if you did not have the log? And the shovel? We just don't need it here.'" The same consultants performed in similar ways when asked to sort other groups. (One group included a shock of wheat, a flower, a tree, and a sickle; another included a plate, a cup, a knife, and a loaf of bread.) These unexpected responses are vivid examples of active, social, functional systems of thinking rather than abstract, categorical thinking. The saw, the axe, and the log belong to a temporal, functional system; the shovel is irrelevant to that system. Because Luria set up his research with Western, categorical, paradigmatic thinking in mind, he mistakenly dismissed the unique systematic thinking used by the Uzbekhi speakers.

The consultants' responses to Luria's syllogism tests showed many similarities to the sorting responses. In these tests Luria gave consultants arguments and asked them to draw conclusions from them (Luria 1971:270). The syllogisms referred either to the concrete, practical experience of the consultants' lives or to unfamiliar things. For example, the syllogism "'Cotton grows where it is hot and humid. In the village it is hot and humid. Does cotton grow there or not?'" was connected directly to the consultants' daily lives. Another syllogism—"'In the North where there is snow all year, the bears are white. Town X is in the North. Are the bears in the town white or not?'"—was one with unfamiliar subject matter.

Luria's subjects dealt easily with the first kind of syllogism, although they did qualify their responses with remarks such as this: "'Well, if the village is warm and humid, then cotton certainly must grow there, of course, if there aren't any hills nearby.'" Consultants refused to draw a conclusion from the second type of syllogism; rather, they denied the major premise. Responses such as the following one were common: "But I don't know what kind of bears are there. I have not been there and I don't want to lie."

Luria's conclusion—that his consultants dealt only at the concrete level and not at the abstract symbolic level—resulted from his assumptions. He was not conducting the study to describe the logic that his consultants displayed and therefore learn about human reasoning. His purpose was to compare his consultants' responses to his own idea of what the responses should be.

In the mid-1960s Michael Cole studied the relation of culture to thought in Liberia (Cole et al. 1971). He also studied the relation of literacy to thought among the Vai (Scribner and Cole 1981). In *The Cultural Context of Learning and Thinking* (Cole et al. 1971) Cole and his co-authors reported an extensive study, conducted among the Kpelle, of various cognitive processes, including classification, learning, memory, and logic. The book addresses the problem of how a "people's thought processes relate to the culture in which they are raised and in which they live." This clearly defined ethnographic pursuit, however, quickly degenerated into an analysis of mistakes made by Kpelle consultants on various psychometric tests. Cole's entire analysis of Kpelle logic rested on the proportions of correct and incorrect responses to logic problems (Cole et al. 1971:176–212). Somehow the ethnographic concern became lost in the tangle of the psychometric methodology.

In their study of Kpelle logic, Cole and his colleagues examined several kinds of data: transcripts of court cases, responses to syllogisms, and responses to logical problems involving conjunction, disjunction, and implication. The data most clearly comparable to Luria's (to be discussed later), and of most interest to us here, concerns syllogisms.

Cole and his colleagues collected all the data in a small isolated Kpelle village reachable by some five hours on foot from the nearest motor road. Thus, according to Cole, the consultants were relatively untainted by contact with Western modes of thought. The research team collected two kinds of data: group and individual responses to logic problems. They recorded all the interviews on magnetic tape for later transcription and analysis. Using a group discussions format, the researchers gave groups of consultants a syllogism, complete with conclusion, and asked them to judge the truth of the conclusion. Individual consultants were given only the premises and were asked to supply the conclusion.

In Cole's terms, in both sets of data some of the responses were correct and some were incorrect. For example, the research team considered the group response to the following problem as correct (Cole et al. 1971:186).

> Experimenter: "Some animals in the bush are black deer. I have seen an animal in the bush. Therefore I saw a black deer."
>
> Response: "No, you have to see that what you saw was a black deer because there are many other animals in the bush, such as red deer and bush hogs."

On the other hand, Cole considered the affirmative responses to the next problem incorrect (Cole et al. 1971:156).

> Experimenter: "Every *Kpelle* man makes rice farms. Some *Kwii* people make rice farms. Therefore, some of the *Kwii* people are *Kpelle*."
>
> Response: Some consultants responded, "Yes, we know that all *Kpelle* men make farms. If anybody makes a rice farm he will be included in the group." Others said, "No, it is true that all *Kpelle* men make rice farms, but there are some *Kwii* people who make rice farms and are not *Kpelle* men. Therefore the statement is not true. Even this white man [John Gay] can make a rice farm, but he is not a *Kpelle* man."

I disagree with Cole's judgment of "incorrect," for in every case consultants drew valid conclusions. This is obvious in the first problem and in the case of those consultants who responded "no" to the second problem. Those who responded "yes" to the second problem, however, also drew valid conclusions. In that case they changed the major premise from "Every *Kpelle* man makes rice farms" to "All men who make rice farms are *Kpelle* men." We may not agree with this premise, but the conclusion does indeed follow from it. Cole and his colleagues should have noted this point.

In *The Psychology of Literacy*, Scribner and Cole (1981) report on a large study of literacy among the Vai of Liberia. Their research sought to describe the interaction between literacy and various cognitive functions. The Vai traditionally participate in three literacies: English, from the colonial period; Arabic, from the Qur'an; and an indigenous Vai script. Cole and Scribner discovered that reading and writing have little effect on higher cognitive functions. The minor effects that they did find showed up mostly in aspects of speech and communication rather than in reasoning. Cole and Scribner found, however, that schooling was very important in determining how people approached logical problems.

Cole and Scribner designed two tests to uncover the relationship between thought and literacy. The first was a series of six simple syllogisms, whose conclusions were given in the form of a question. For example:

> All houses in Liberia are made of iron.
> My friend has a house in Liberia.
> Is my friend's house made of iron?

The second test replicated two of the original six syllogisms, but substituted unfamiliar content (men on the moon and blue rocks). Consultants were asked to respond "yes" or "no" to the questions and to explain their answers. Cole and Scribner scored the responses according to two criteria: responses could be correct or incorrect, and the explanations could be empirical (expressed through real-world knowledge) or theoretical (expressed through the information given in the problem).

Scribner and Cole present little discussion of the responses, so I cannot address their data. Their goal, however, was not to describe Vai reasoning patterns, but to document, and perhaps explain, differences between Vai and Western patterns. If they had sought to describe Vai patterns, they would have elicited very different data. They would have constructed their test syllogisms from Vai semantic fields, and they would have presented their respondents with a wide range of syllogisms so they could expose the underlying rules for drawing conclusions.

For the past ten years or so I have collected syllogistic data in four major language families: Indo-European (English), Algonquian (Ojibwa), Athabascan (Navajo), and Mande-kan (Mende). In each case I used the same methods to collect my data, so the data are comparable across cases. Furthermore, my methods were close enough to Luria's and Cole's that I can compare their data to mine.

I elicited syllogistic data using a three-step process. First I elicited from my consultants a set of words, in which each word related to others in the set with "kind of" semantics ("*A* is a kind of *B*"). This set served as the semantic basis of the data-collection protocol. When I began this work, as I mentioned in chapter 1, I thought of this set as a folk taxonomy; at that time most cognitive anthropologists accepted the folk taxonomy as a relatively accurate representation of how people conceived their world. Since then, however, some scholars have come to realize that nothing as simple and as primitive as a taxonomy can hope to capture the complexities of human semantic systems. They are beginning to think of meaning as an interaction among various features such as "kind of," "part of," "caused by," and "is used for." These features operate at all levels of a semantic system, from the level of concrete objects and behaviors to the level involving abstract principles of interpretation.

In Werner and Schoepfle's words (1987:96), the focus has shifted from "looking for the *universal building blocks* of human knowledge" to seeking "the *universal mortar* that holds together the language-specific building blocks" (authors' emphasis). This change in view has had no effect on my syllogism research, which uses only taxonomic ("kind of") meanings rather than whole folk taxonomies. Furthermore, I do not believe that folk taxonomies represent how people actually conceptualize their world. I use the "kind of" meaning not as some component of a larger lexical structure but as a universal lexical/semantic relationship that can connect any two words.

In the second step of the research I used the taxonomy to develop a group of sentences that expressed, in the native language, various class-inclusion relationships. I combined these sentences to form all of the syllogisms required by classical logic. Finally, I presented the consultants with all of the syllogisms.

My analysis of their responses shows that the consultants never drew an invalid conclusion. This is not to say that the syllogism, as found in logic textbooks, describes how all people think; it does not. Like the folk taxonomy, the syllogism is far too simplistic and too rigid.

As with Cole's study, some of the conclusions that appeared invalid proved to be valid upon further investigation. For example, a Mende-speaking consultant said, "No cows are sows," as a conclusion to this syllogism:

> Major premise: Some pigs are sows.
> Minor premise: No cows are pigs.

This conclusion looks incorrect, but when the consultant was asked to argue to the conclusion, he responded:

> All sows are pigs.
> No cows are pigs.
> Therefore no cows are sows.

In this syllogism the conclusion follows because the consultant changed the major premise. This act of changing the premise is not unusual. Cole's consultants changed premises, Luria's consultants rejected his major premise, and similar premise-changing occurred in every language that I studied (Hamill 1979).

Table 2-1 gives examples of some of the premise changes I observed. Note that each conclusion the consultants drew followed from changed premises. Two basic kinds of change are apparent here. In direct change, the consultant alters the content of the premise. For example, in the Navajo syllogism the consultant changed "Some plants are not trees" to "Some plants are trees." The other kind of change is

Table 2-1
Examples of Premise Changes

	Original Syllogism	Change
Ojibwa		
Major premise:	Some fish are not pike.	All fish are living things.
Minor premise:	All fish are living things.	All pike are fish.
	Conclusion: All pike are living things.	
English		
Major premise:	All toy cars are toys.	Some toy cars are matchbox racers.
Minor premise:	Some toy cars are matchbox racers.	All toy cars are toys.
	Conclusion: Some toys are matchbox racers.	
Navajo		
Major premise:	No grasses are trees.	No grasses are trees.
Minor premise:	Some plants are not trees.	Some plants are trees.
	Conclusion: Some plants are not grasses.	

an alteration in premise order. The six-year-old English-speaking consultant changed the major premise to the minor premise and the minor to the major. Both basic kinds of change occurred in the Ojibwa example.

Any theory in ethno-logic must account for the fact that consultants draw valid conclusions when presented with these tests, and it somehow must include rules for drawing conclusions from categorical arguments. If drawing valid conclusions were the entire story, we could account for the data using the rules developed by logicians. More complete data on syllogisms, however, show that those rules overpredict. Certain kinds of conclusions allowed under the textbook-logic view of the syllogism are often rejected by consultants. These conclusions always involve particular statements for which the corresponding universal statement also is true. For example, "Some sows are animals" (all sows are) and "Some cedars are plants" (all cedars are). In my work, all consultants rejected this type of conclusion even when the rejected conclusion was valid under textbook rules.

Any account of human reasoning must explain two aspects of these results. First, it must explain why all consultants rejected this type of particular conclusion, where the universal statement is also true. To say that these rejections are errors and that the primitive mind is concrete or preoperative or prelogical explains nothing. Ethno-logic, however, can explain this phenomenon by pointing to the semantic relationships that make up the syllogism. Syllogisms argue about categories or classes of things related taxonomically. In the textbook view of the syllogism, "some" means "there exist" or "at least one," but in natural language "some" refers to a partial intersection of a dominant category with a subordinate category. That is, "some" implies a taxonomic relationship ("some trees are oaks"). Thus the arguments that led to these rejected conclusions violated the natural-language semantics of "some."

Second, the account must explain why these conclusions were rejected in all languages. Again, the taxonomic semantic relationship serves to explain the problem. Although the taxonomic relationship is only a small part of culture and language, it belongs to all cultures and languages. "Kind of" is a semantic universal; it exists in all languages and expresses relations among things that are important to all cultures. Thus one would expect to find universal rejection of the arguments that lead to conclusions that violate taxonomic semantics. This view of reasoning patterns accounts for the data without resorting to the assertion that consultants were making mistakes.

If meaning gives structure to human reasoning, semantic universals will accompany universals in logical patterns. Thus the model integrates ethnosemantics with ethno-logic. It also provides a specific research strategy for continued investigation.

Semantics and Logic

The semantic account of human reasoning states that people establish logical conclusions based on the semantic structure of arguments. Linking reasoning patterns to meaning structures explains both universal and culture-specific findings. The semantic account suggests new areas of study that can test its truth and explains the large body of data that is now available. Even so, methods designed to test this theory must ensure that the data are complete and are elicited from native semantic fields.

Because the syllogism is popular in ethno-logical research, large quantities of syllogistic data are available in the literature. These data exhibit certain common properties. In all of the studies to date, consultants have changed or rejected premises and rejected certain valid conclusions. At the same time, it is difficult to find consultants who drew invalid conclusions. Indeed, all of the conclusions that Luria and Cole report were drawn validly. In some cases the rules of logic that consultants used appear to be stricter than the ones followed by textbook logic. Because many of these consultants are primitives (according to many of the researchers), the syllogistic data weaken the colonialist viewpoint so much that we need not consider it further.

The homogeneity of responses to syllogistic tests also weakens the extreme relativist view. Syllogistic data come from a wide variety of languages and cultures, but in every research case all conclusions are drawn validly and in every language the same kinds of conclusions are rejected. If logical processing were totally an artifact of language or of culture, these commonalities would not appear. Such commonalities may be properties of any or all thinking systems, or they may distinguish humans from other thinking beings. In either case, all people share some basic thinking patterns.

Studies of propositional reasoning, however, deny the conclusion that logic has the same structure regardless of language or culture. In syllogistic reasoning, categories of objects are related so that valid conclusions can be drawn. In propositional reasoning, validity is keyed to logical operators that combine declarative sentences. Consider this statement:

(1) The gopher chased the mouse or bit the snake.

In English this sentence would be true in three cases: (1) the gopher chased the mouse, (2) the gopher bit the snake, or (3) the gopher did both. Because the entire sentence is true in each of these three cases, I cannot conclude that the gopher chased the mouse. Yet, if I say

(2) The gopher chased the mouse and bit the snake,

I can conclude that the gopher chased the mouse because in English the second sentence is true only if both of the conjuncts are true.

When I elicited the truth conditions for the English sentence given in sentence (2) from a group of bilingual Navajo speakers, they all agreed with the English logic. In their view the English sentence was true only if the gopher both chased the mouse and bit the snake. Then I asked them to translate the sentence into Navajo, and I elicited the truth conditions of the Navajo sentence. Each consultant responded that the Navajo sentence was true only if the right-hand portion of the sentence were true; that is, only if the gopher bit the snake. The logic of the sentence changed when it was translated from English to Navajo. This example shows clearly how a strictly universalist view of human reasoning cannot account for the data.

The semantic account explains both the syllogistic and the propositional data. It explains why consultants respond to syllogisms in the same way worldwide: the "kind of" semantic relationship is a universal aspect of language that relates words and gives structure to some reasoning. On the other hand, aspects of meaning that are peculiar to specific languages and cultures will produce propositional reasoning patterns that differ in some respects from language to language.

Thus a semantic view of reasoning can account for both universal and culture-specific logical patterns. If the model is left at that, however, it is too loose. Researchers who find culture-specific logical patterns could claim that those patterns derive from culture-specific semantic structures. If that were the case, any and all patterns could be valid, and the semantic account would be untestable. To withstand this criticism, the semantic account must claim that all meaning is either a realization of a semantic universal or is derived from a combination of underlying semantic universals.

The taxonomic relationship is not the only semantic universal. Anthropologists working in ethnosemantics have proposed several sets of universal semantic relationships. All of these sets have in common the idea that all lexical meaning is derived from primitive semantic relationships. The sets differ only in the abstractness of the relationships they propose. The least abstract consist of "lexical/semantic" relationships that are expressed easily in natural language.

Table 2-2
Lexical/Semantic Universals

Relationship		
Spradley	Casagrande and Hale	Meaning
inclusion	inclusion	X is a kind of Y
space		X is a part of Y
		X is a place in Y
	space	X is oriented with respect to Y
cause-effect	contingency	X is contingent on Y
rational	operational	X is a reason for doing Y
location		X is a place for doing Y
function		X is used for Y
means-end	function	X is a means of effecting Y
sequence	grading	X is in a sequence including Y
attribution	attributive	X is a characteristic of Y
	comparison	X is similar to or different from Y
	exemplification	X is an example of Y
	synonymy	X is equivalent to Y
	antonymy	X is the opposite of Y
	provenance	X is the source of Y
	circularity	X is X

Casagrande and Hale (1967:168) and Spradley (1981:93) exemplify this tactic. Their universal semantic relationships are shown in table 2-2. These two lists are identical for the most part; it would not be difficult to translate one into the other.

The meanings of words are derived from the primitives on these lists by means of compounding. For example, Casagrande and Hale (1967:167) found that the meaning of the Papago word *da:k* (nose) was derived by combining a spatial relationship (that which stands beneath our eyes) with an operational relationship (from which we breathe).

The other strategy is more abstract. It is not intended to derive the meanings of words, but is used to derive lexical/semantic relationships like those in table 2-2. Werner and Topper (1976) and Werner and Schoepfle (1987) propose three semantic universals: M (Modification), T (Taxonomy), and Q (Sequence). From these they derive lexical/semantic relationships such as part-whole. In another formulation, Schoepfle, Burton, and Morgan (1984:266) identify "taxonomy," "sequence," and "implication" as the "most elemental relations between terms."

Each of these semantic relationships has its own logic; that is, each contains argument structures that lead to valid conclusions. Future research in ethno-logic should take advantage of those structures and determine whether they are the same in a wide variety of language and culture settings. If the semantic model is correct, we should expect to observe similar patterns of validity in all of the languages and cultures we study. If we do not, the theory fails.

Research in ethno-logic should study the structure of arguments in rigid paradigmatic designs. These studies can be used as a means to understand reasoning in natural discourse. Natural discourse studies are clearly more important than studies of structural validity; people do not argue in tightly structured logical formats even if such a format stands behind what they do. Yet, just as anthropologists cannot understand the workings of a clan without a grasp of its structure, they cannot understand what is going on in a conversation without a firm knowledge of the structures that underlie it. Studies of structural validity will establish those argument forms that are permissible in any language or culture. In that context we can examine how people actually reason in their everyday lives.

Any study of structural validity must be conducted in keeping with the worldview of the study's subjects. Reason advances in a sea of truth; people think in terms that they believe and understand and that are real to them. Thus if the premises that make up a data-collection protocol are not true from the native's point of view, the conclusions that may or may not follow from the premises will have little meaning.

Studies of structural validity also require that research consultants respond to complete logical paradigms. The first goal of an ethno-logical study is to describe the logic (or logics) employed by the native speaker. Not all possible reasoning structures behave in the same way; some structures lead to conclusions, whereas others do not. One of the first steps in researching the pattern is to compile an inventory of structures that lead to conclusions and one of structures that do not. The processes that generate patterns of conclusions and nonconclusions are not described unless the descriptions generate all of the pattern and only the pattern. To find out what all of the pattern is, one must present consultants with all of the paradigm. When researchers give consultants complete paradigms, generated from the consultants' worldview, they can identify reasoning errors that the consultants' knowledge system defines. Then they can begin to describe the processes that make patterns of valid and invalid logical structures.

The Use of Error in the Study of Meaning   3

Nobody is perfect. All people make mistakes in almost every area of their lives. They misspell words; they speak and write ungrammatical sentences; they mistake one thing for another; they violate rules of etiquette and decorum. In fact, mistakes occur in all areas of life where mistakes are possible. An error is not a failure; when a bone is overstressed and fractures, it fails, but it is not in error. For an act to be an error, it must contradict some principle. Errors are ideological, not physical.

No person living in any given culture is any more or less prone to error than any person living in another culture. Certainly the character of mistakes is a product of a particular culture—what is correct in one cultural setting is often incorrect in another—but mistakes are not a result of the way in which people live. Mistakes occur because people know what their way of life is. This knowledge is not always explicit, however; people are not always able to discuss what they know. Nonetheless, they use what they know to make the worlds, the meanings, in which they live. If people could not create meanings as they use their knowledge, they could not make mistakes.

Things that do not possess knowledge cannot make mistakes. Such things respond to the natural forces in their environment but do not assign a value to the response. Yet the possession of knowledge alone is not enough for error to exist. The ability to create meaning and to assign it to everyday life events is also necessary. A rock, a tree, or a computer is incapable of making a mistake because it lacks the power to assign meaning to anything. On the other hand, grasshoppers, fish, chimpanzees, and other creatures capable of assigning meaning probably can err. Mistakes are made in an instant of time by people acting within their systems of knowledge.

Errors are tied to judgments about relationships between acts and ideas. Mistakes do not depend on the properties of events themselves but derive from the interaction of mind and event. Thus in many ways my concept of mistakes is similar to Mary Douglas's concept of dirt, which was part of her study on taboo (Douglas 1966:40). Douglas defines dirt as disorder—as matter that is out of place. She asserts that people react to dirt, ambiguity, and anomaly in much the same ways: they ignore, condemn, or create new reality (Douglas 1966:37–40). Similarly, social scientists can use errors as data that reveal the knowledge systems that make up culture.

Error is, therefore, a powerful methodological tool, but it has gone largely unnoticed in social theories that explain action in terms of external causes—in structural functionalism and conflict theory in sociology and in cultural materialism in anthropology. The reason for this oversight is much like the reason why these theories misjudge reasoning patterns: they explain culture in terms of forces that are outside the person. Thus social scientists can assume that all people think alike without regard to language and culture; they regard people's mistakes as mere isolated cases having little to do with theory. In these terms the only important mistakes are those that social scientists make in their studies.

If social theory explains culture by focusing on what people know, it also assumes that people know more than they make explicit. That is, there are tacit knowledge systems that account for what people do. Error then can provide an important opportunity for understanding those systems. Douglas's work and most of the arguments in generative linguistics exemplify how anthropologists can take advantage of this opportunity. Errors are important in social science research, whether researchers or subjects make them and whether they result from ignorance or from design. Yet errors will remain insignificant if researchers ignore them.

By their nature, errors can occur only when meaning contradicts knowledge. The fact that people make mistakes shows that they assign meanings to the events in their lives and that they compare those meanings to standards, values, and expectations in their minds. Error, like ungrammatical sentences or dirt, is therefore a window to the mind and a strong methodological tool for uncovering the basic knowledge systems that make up culture.

Generative linguists use ungrammatical sentences to expose the linguistic processes, both universal and particular, that make up our knowledge of language. Ethno-logic uses a similar method because validity is a feature of logical systems; that is, for a system to possess a logic, some argument structures must not lead to conclusions. Thus, when complete patterns of valid and invalid arguments are studied, it is possible to define the tacit logical systems that people use.

The Ins and Outs of Social Theory

A theory in the social sciences must account for social activity, such as political or economic behavior, in abstract concepts. Such theories are well and good as far as they go; they parallel theories in the physical sciences such as physics and biology and inspire confidence in western Europeans. They diverge from those theories, however, in the content of their abstract concepts.

Whereas physics assumes that force or heat are as real as rocks, the social sciences place no such constraint on abstract concepts. Some of these concepts are statistical fictions. For example, sociologists define a social class by the aggregate attributes of the people who make it up. The concept does not claim that any one member of a class actually has any or all of those attributes, nor does it claim that if an individual has the attributes he or she is a member of that class.

Other concepts are tautological. Cultural materialism defines infrastructure as the material basis of culture. On this basis cultures develop their structural (economic and political) forms and their superstructural (ideology and ritual) identities (Harris 1979:55–58). That is, infrastructures determine the form and content of cultures. Yet because the nature of any particular infrastructure is defined in both structural and superstructural terms, the dragon eats its tail. Infrastructure becomes an empty concept because it is impossible to imagine a real world where one cannot identify an infrastructure. French structuralism suffers from the same problem because it assumes that people think in dualisms. Dichotomies are such powerful formal devices that it is impossible to imagine a situation that a researcher could not analyze as a dual organization. Under both French structuralism and cultural materialism, it is impossible to determine the reality of basic concepts. They could be artifacts of the world, artifacts of theorizing, or both.

If the source of social life is individual knowledge, culture consists of what a person knows. Cultural universals are things that all people know; people are born with them, and specific cultural forms are derived from them. These universals do not have their source outside people in a mechanistic response to an impersonal environment. Instead, like a Chomskian language acquisition device, they are a property of human beings. People come into the world with innate knowledge about culture, and they use that knowledge to interact with their environment and to acquire the specifics of their own culture. From this point of view, every feature of culture is derived from this innate base. Thus this base lies at the heart of the general theory of culture.

The generative linguists employ this model productively in the study of language, but to do so they must rely on error. The fact that sentence (1) below is well formed in English tells nothing about why it is well formed.

(1) The boy bit the dog.

When the ungrammatical example in sentence (2) is considered, however, the parts of the sentence that contribute to grammaticality begin to emerge.

(2) *Boy the bit the dog. [* means "ungrammatical string"]

In fact no corpus composed only of well-formed language strings, no matter how large, can reveal the grammatical constituents of any utterance in any language. When linguists juxtapose grammatical strings with ungrammatical strings, they can study the structural components of the language. When they consider several languages at once, they can study the composition and structure of the general components of language. They can begin to describe the innate knowledge that allows people to learn language.

Douglas used similar juxtapositions in her study on taboo in which she defined dirt as matter out of place. She contrasted the "dirty" with the "clean" in several different cultural settings and used this contrast to contribute significant insights to our concept of taboo. Douglas also clarified both the cognitive status of primitive religion and our ideas concerning the evolution of religion when she noted that all dirty things are clean in another setting. Thus nothing is intrinsically dirty; dirt is a matter of location. Douglas noted that people associate dirt with pollution and pollution with danger. Therefore she was able to explain such taboo complexes as the abominations of Leviticus (Douglas 1966:41–57) in terms of a worldview. In Levitican terms the inhabitants of the water are scaly, like fish. Accordingly, things without scales that live in the water, such as shellfish, are living in the wrong place and are dirty.

Two aspects of this argument deserve attention. The first is that the concept of dirt is much like the linguist's notion of an ungrammatical string. Dirt is not dirty because it is dirty; it is dirty because it is out of place—because it is "ungrammatical" matter. The second interesting aspect concerns Douglas's assumptions about human beings. She assumes that certain meanings are human in scope and are expressed in all cultures. She also assumes that people create their social life (Douglas 1966:2).

If Douglas had argued that the concept of dirt accounted for only the western European view of taboo, then her work would have amounted to nothing more than literary criticism. Instead, she discusses people in general and thus makes a genuine contribution to our understanding of religion. If this contribution is to carry any weight, one must assume that dirt, matter, and place are general human concepts, not restricted to any particular language or culture. Furthermore, one must assume that all humans sometimes associate dirt with impurity and therefore with danger and taboo. Douglas is not merely writing about dirt; she is making claims about the structure of the mind. Furthermore, she does not restrict those claims to the mere association of words with meanings. The fact that there is a place for matter to be "out of" implies a theory of order held by the individual. Place is a complex notion in this sense because it defines relationships between things rather than the things themselves. Douglas's work is important not because people *can* associate things with place but because they *must*.

Douglas's ideas not only require people to carry certain meanings and to have certain kinds of ideas; they also imply that people create with meanings and ideas. Without meaning nothing can be out of place or in place. Before something can be regarded as out of place, people must compare the meaning of the thing to their knowledge about its place in their theory of order. Furthermore, they must make the comparison whenever it is appropriate. Because most, if not all, situations are novel, the labeling of something as dirty is an act of creation. Constantly, and of necessity, we create the dirt (the world) around us.

The assumptions that underlie Douglas's work demonstrate an important flaw in most social theory. Douglas assumes that people create their social lives; she does not try to account for social life by referring to abstract external forces. In contrast, most social theorists exclude the individual from any part in the creation of social life. I believe that they make this mistake out of a desire to emulate the successes of the physical sciences, combined with an unclear notion of what the physical sciences actually study. When physical scientists conduct research, they are not simply studying matter or its behavior. Rather, they are trying to explain why the matter behaves as it does in terms of properties of the matter (which are often unobservable). Thus gravity is a real property of matter, although it cannot be directly observed.

Many social scientists demand that hypotheses only deal with directly observable human behavior. This approach ties social theory to behavior and excludes meaning because scientists cannot observe meaning. Within the confines of this approach the only possible accounts of social life are statistical fictions, such as class, or tautologies, such as infrastructure.

In the search for scientific respectability, the social sciences lost sight of the goal of explaining social life. Many scholars adhere to an unwritten rule that one cannot account for what people do in terms of human nature. To do so would require reference to knowledge that is held individually and is unobservable. Yet social scientists can reject this value and accept the countervalue that they must account for human social life in human terms. In that case the locus of social theory would be the structure of the human mind. Accordingly, the abstract concepts mentioned in social theories would be creations of human thought, and universals of culture would represent universal human meanings.

By accepting the idea that, to a large extent, social forces are located in each individual and that social activity must be explained with reference to people, the social sciences would move toward a clearer understanding of the nature of social processes. The concepts put forward to explain social life according to this view are structures in the mind. By the same token, semantic particulars must be derivatives of semantic universals, which represent the innate knowledge that allows humans to acquire culture. Semantic structures are abstract representations of meanings and relationships between meanings. The fact of error provides both a clue to the nature of human semantic systems and a method for studying them. Error does not cause creativity because many of the acts and events that people create are not mistakes. Rather, error is an index or sign of creativity. It implies a system of knowledge in which something is a mistake. Thus, just as linguists learn about the internal workings of language from studies of ungrammatical strings, social scientists learn about culture from the study of error.

Error and Method

Many social scientists ignore error as a methodological tool—a choice that is not surprising in view of the dominance of theories that propose external forces to explain social life in mainstream thought. If people really were in the thrall of social forces beyond their control, they could not make mistakes of interest to social science. Because people create their lives, the study of error becomes a powerful means of exploring the knowledge with which people make community life.

The scientific research paradigm contains two possible loci of error: either the researcher or the subject. Discussions of both types of mistakes exist in the literature. The extensive debate in sociology on the use of negative evidence (Denzin 1970; Lewis and Lewis 1980; Sjoberg and Nett 1968) includes a thorough discussion of methodological errors. At issue was whether qualitative or quantitative methods were best suited for considering negative evidence. In anthropology, accounts of error by the researcher can be found in most good ethnographies, which often devote some space to "mistakes I made in the field." Until recently, these accounts made up almost all the anthropological writing about ethnographic field methods. Discussions of mistakes made by subjects or consultants are less common than discussions of researchers' errors but do appear in the literature. Some of this material explains how people deal with the mistakes that they and others make (Hughes 1951; Riemer 1976), and some studies use native error to study the underlying knowledge system that makes an act an error (Cole et al. 1971; Douglas 1966).

In one of the more recent rounds in the sociological debate over negative evidence, some sociologists took a renewed interest in qualitative research methods. Advocates of both qualitative and quantitative methods agreed that social scientists must consider and deal with evidence that may refute one's own theoretical ideas. Each side asserted that its methods were the best for gathering negative evidence and that the other method was weak in this regard. Lewis and Lewis approached the topic explicitly and concluded that "quantitative methods offer the best and most reliable research design for guaranteeing that negative evidence be considered" (1980:556). Earlier, Becker (1958) built negative evidence into the final stage of field analysis—the construction of social system models. In this final stage researchers can use negative evidence to increase the accuracy of the social models they developed in previous stages (Becker 1958:653–58).

Fortunately, the debate failed in its manifest purpose of identifying which type of method best ensured that the researcher would consider negative evidence. Ultimately the only conclusion that could be reached was that researchers, not methods, fail to consider negative evidence. Yet the debate succeeded in making social scientists aware of the importance of negative evidence, and it introduced new ways of discovering and using negative evidence.

Similar benefits emerged from the "mistakes I made in the field" literature, which once characterized scholarly work in anthropological field methods. "The field" in anthropology carries the mystical quality of a rite of passage and therefore involves more than mere scientific method. The field is profoundly moving and must be experienced personally. For this reason, many anthropologists have avoided any attempt to make ethnography's methodology explicit. (One post–World War II anthropologist, who asked his major professor for training in field methods, was told to be sure to take a lot of dime novels and marmalade.) More recently, however, some anthropologists have attempted to demystify the field, making explicit, sophisticated statements of what researchers can do in the field (Agar 1980; Pelto 1970; Spradley 1981). These statements, however, are often expanded examples of the "mistakes I made in the field" genre couched in positivistic prose—good wine in bad bottles.

For much of anthropology's history the best place to find information on ethnographic field methods was in the ethnographies themselves. There scholars discussed the problems they encountered and the mistakes they made in the field. Their colleagues then could judge the quality of the evidence they presented. In this way we know that Evans-Pritchard believed mistakenly that among the Azandi, cynicism concerning their witches and oracles implied disbelief (Evans-Pritchard 1937:183–201). We also know that Chagnon believed his consultants' lies about their ancestors (Chagnon 1983:18–20).

Unlike the negative evidence debate among sociologists, the anthropologists' debate was never intended to resolve competition among methods. Yet, like the negative evidence debate, it did lead to improvements in ethnographic techniques. Anthropologists assumed that they would make mistakes in the field and they used their predecessors' reports of field errors as forewarning.

Today researchers recognize errors (in the sense of meaning denying knowledge) as one of the important epistemological tools available to the field worker. Agar (1986:20–39) structures his view of field methods in terms of breakdowns that violate ethnographers' assumptions of coherence. Werner and Schoepfle (1987:57–68) identify "anomaly" as the key to the use of "epistemological windows."

The second locus of error in the research paradigm is the subject. Social scientists are understandably reluctant to label what their subjects do a mistake. Not only is such labeling pretentious, but, in the light of external social theory, it also weakens their evidence and calls their conclusions into doubt. Fortunately, however, this reluctance has not deterred all work on mistakes that subjects make. The literature contains interesting accounts that tell of how people deal with error in their lives and (as noted above) tell what error reveals about the underlying knowledge that makes an error an error.

Hughes (1951) studied errors made by tradesmen working on

building projects and found not only that construction mistakes were relatively common but also that construction workers organized building mistakes by trade. Carpenters blamed electricians, electricians blamed plumbers, and so on. Riemer (1976) replicated Hughes's work, confirming his conclusions and adding to our understanding of the issue. Studies such as these demonstrate how people define and react to error. Yet they do not realize the full research potential of error because they ignore its value in revealing the structure and content of underlying knowledge.

Douglas's analysis of dirt, purity, and taboo is a good example of how to use error to reveal cultural knowledge. In her argument Douglas defined dirt, and the labeling of things as dirty, in terms of a theory of order held by individuals. She demonstrated the value of this theory by accounting for known taboo complexes through known worldviews. Douglas also reasoned in the other direction and used known inventories of dirt and taboo to investigate worldviews. Her arguments are compelling; they may assume universal, and therefore innate, meanings (e.g., dirt) and relationships of meaning (e.g., worldviews, theories of order). Douglas does not discuss this issue, however, so it is impossible to tell whether she is working from this or some other body of assumption.

Generative linguists, in their use of error, assume universals of structural meanings (e.g., verb phrase, noun phrase) and of relationships between structural meanings (e.g., subject, predicate, object). John Ross's (1970) classic argument on gapping and the order of constituents demonstrates the explanatory power embodied in these assumptions. Gapping occurs in all languages when two or more sentences, each containing an identical constituent, are combined. For example, one can combine sentences (3) and (4) to make (5) and (6).

(3) I ate fish.
(4) Bill ate rice.
(5) I ate fish and Bill ate rice.
(6) I ate fish and Bill rice.

Sentences (5) and (6) are the same except that the second "ate" is not present in (6). That deletion is an example of gapping.

Gapping does not occur in the same places in all languages. Sentence (7) is sentence (6) translated into Japanese. (Note that "prt" stands for participle.)

(7) *watakusi wa sakana o, Biru wa gohan o tabeta.*
    I   (prt)fish (prt)Bill (prt) rice   (prt)ate.

Table 3-1
Constituent Order and Gapping

A. SVO + SO . . . forward gapping	
B. SOV + SO . . .	" "
C. SO + . . . + SO + SOV backward gapping	
D. *SO + . . . + SO + SVO	" "

Source: Ross 1970:255.

Note that in Japanese the first "ate" was deleted rather than the second. Ross argued that the order of gapping in a language depended on the order in which major constituents (subject, object, and verb in this case) appear in the sentence. In English the order of constituents is subject, verb, object (SVO); in Japanese the order is subject, object, verb (SOV). English exhibits forward gapping, which can be expressed in a rule such as R(1): SVO + SVO ⇒ SVO + SO. Japanese exhibits backward gapping, which can be expressed in R(2): SOV + SOV ⇒ SO + SOV. There are four possible combinations of constituent order (SVO and SOV) and gapping direction (forward and backward) (see table 3-1).

Ross noted that three of these four combinations can be found in some language but that the fourth (D) cannot. That is, no SVO languages (such as English) gap backward (Ross 1970:255), and in no language is sentence (8) grammatical.

(8) *I fish and Bill ate rice.

Ross also noted that some languages exhibit only one form of gapping: English shows only type A, and Japanese only type C. Some other languages, however, show more than one type because of scrambling, a common linguistic process that "optionally permutes major elements of a clause" (Ross 1970:251–52). Russian, for example, allows scrambling, and it exhibits all three possible forms of gapping. Ross surveyed the world's languages for examples of each of the "eight logically possible subsets of these first three . . . types" (Ross 1970:255). Table 3-2 summarizes his findings.

Ross had to explain why sentence (8) is ungrammatical in any language and why no language exhibits only B, only AB, or only AC patterns. He solved the problem by proposing two statements to be added to the general theory of language (Ross 1970:257):

> A. The order in which gapping operates depends on the order of the elements at the time that the rule applies; if the identical elements are on left branches, gapping operates forward; if they are on right branches, it operates backward . . . and gapping is an

Table 3-2
Gapping Types by Language

*None	Only A	*Only B	Only C
	English		Japanese
	French		Siouan

*Only AB	*Only AC	BC	ABC
		Hindi	Russian
		Turkish	Latin

Source: Ross 1970:256.

"anywhere" rule, that is, it can apply anywhere in the derivation of a sentence.

B. If a language has SOV order in the deep structure, it is a verb-final language: its grammar can contain no rule which moves the verb to the left.

The distributions in tables 3-1 and 3-2 follow from these two statements. In languages that do not scramble, only A gapping patterns (for SVO languages) and C gapping patterns (for SOV languages) are possible. Languages that scramble exhibit multiple gapping patterns, thus explaining why there are no "only-B" gapping languages.

Type D in table 3-1, of which sentence (8) is an example, is blocked because its only possible derivation violates principle B. Derivation (1) shows the only possible order to apply gapping and scrambling so that sentence (8) can be derived:

$$\text{D(1) SOV + SOV} \xrightarrow{\text{forward gapping}} \text{SO + SOV} \xrightarrow{\text{scrambling}} \text{*SO + SVO}$$

That is, according to the scrambling rule, the verb would have to move to the left. Such a move is explicitly forbidden in SOV languages by the second principle. The generation of "only AB" and "only AC" languages also is blocked by Ross's principles. "Only AB" languages can only come from SVO languages that gap before scrambling but not after. "Only AC" languages can only come from languages that gap after scrambling but not before. Because gapping is an "anywhere" rule, languages cannot restrict its application in this way (Ross 1970:256).

I have discussed Ross's ideas here not because gapping and scrambling are important social concepts but because of the structure of Ross's argument. Ross claims that all human beings are born with innate knowledge, which is captured in ideas such as SOV, SVO, subject, object, verb, and gapping. On the basis of this claim he accounts for important aspects of the syntax of all SVO and SOV languages (which may comprise all languages). He also clears up some troubling questions about the Indo-European language group (Ross 1970:258–59).

Knowing how languages scramble and gap carries little fascination for social scientists, but the claim of universally held knowledge is of interest to them. Ross's work and many other works by generative linguists make this claim, and they do so under the restrictions exemplified in Ross's work. Yet such a claim demands specific explanation; it is not enough for Ross to claim a relationship between word order and the direction of gapping. He must state exactly what the relationship is. Moreover, the principles behind such a claim must be testable, and in Ross's case they are easily proven wrong. Finally, the principles must be independently motivated; they must be useful in more than one problem area. Ross does meet this requirement; his principles not only account for how languages gap but also help to account for the basic structure of all Indo-European languages. Hypotheses meeting the conditions just listed are both strong (they are easily tested) and powerful (they account for a great deal).

Error plays a central part in linguistic arguments because knowledge of language is covert and expresses itself in creative ways. No one can state all the knowledge that makes up one's native tongue or all the knowledge that allows one to learn it; they are below the conscious level and can be retrieved only through research. Yet the research is hampered by the fact that almost every instance of language use, either production or interpretation, is novel. We create the meanings we express with language as we use the language. This situation makes it difficult to collect comparative data because each sentence is new and different. Fortunately, the research does not seek to explain the existence of the sentences but is intended to represent the knowledge that generates them. In this regard, the fact of error demonstrates the existence of the knowledge. The composition of the errors reveals the structure and content of the knowledge. The same is true of culture.

Culture's empirical reality is knowledge. This knowledge is held individually, but it derives from innate, and therefore universal, knowledge. This knowledge is not a static inventory of informational items but a process that adjusts meanings to contexts. It gives people the ability to create their culture as they live their lives. Error is a window on the form and the content of that knowledge, but these two components are intertwined intricately. Therefore it is impossible to understand one outside the context of the other. Meaning is not distinct from the structure of any reasoning pattern; it is part of that structure.

The Uses of Error in Participant Observation

Both errors of ignorance and errors of purpose have their place in social theory and method. Errors of ignorance are made when the individual making the error is unaware of the underlying knowledge that makes a particular act an error. Errors of purpose occur when the individual acts with full knowledge that the act is an error. Neither kind of error can be used to its fullest in research without the knowledge of social systems that comes from participant observation.

Sociology and anthropology differ in their concept of participant observation. In anthropology it is a method whose goal is to represent the world from the natives' viewpoint (Malinowski 1922:25; Spradley 1981:3–5). In traditional formulations, when culture was taken to mean shared knowledge and behavior, the world to be represented was taken to be the world that the natives shared. As the concept of culture evolved to recognize intracultural variability, so did participant observation. As a result, ethnographies now include accounts of intracultural variation, metacultural schemata, and intentionality (Werner and Schoepfle 1987:79–88). Throughout this evolution, participant observation has required that the researcher participate in the daily life of the community for an extended period (typically a year or more). During this time the researcher augments observations with interviews that range from casual to the highly structured. Since the goal of the method is to describe the natives' point of view, participant observation is almost never oriented toward problematic issues or relationships between theoretical concepts. Those subjects are left to comparative approaches in anthropology.

Sociologists use participant observation when they "are especially interested in understanding a particular organization or substantive problem rather than demonstrating relations between abstractly defined variables" (Becker 1958:652–53). As in anthropology, the focus here is descriptive. Unlike the case in anthropology, however, participant observation in sociology seeks to describe phenomena from the researcher's point of view rather than from the natives'. This is a slight difference, more obvious in theory than in practice. It may account for anthropologists' greater emphasis on interviews and the analysis of interview data and also for sociologists' greater use of research conducted without the subjects' knowledge.

Both researchers and natives make mistakes, either on purpose or out of ignorance. Researchers in the field often are unaware of the social rules at work in the system under study and thus make mistakes. Field workers, especially linguists, often present natives with errors that they generate on purpose as an effective way to test their ideas about native knowledge. Natives' errors of ignorance are especially important in the process of enculturation or socialization. In addition, natives can and do violate the rules of the social system to elicit certain responses from their culturemates. All of these kinds of error are important sources of ethnographic information.

In the field, researchers live in cultures to which they are not native, thus experiencing a discontinuity between expectation and response. The field worker acts in certain ways, and often expects responses, that do not reflect what the natives do. In other words, the researcher's expectations differ from those of the natives. Expectations derive in turn from culture—that is, from knowledge. Therefore this sort of discontinuity shows where researchers' and natives' knowledge differs. It provides information that the researcher can use to explore the knowledge system under study.

There are important similarities and connections between the researcher in the field and the child learning culture. Both operate in relative ignorance of the social rules used by the people around them. Also, both have the goal of learning those rules and of acquiring the appropriate knowledge. The child also brings some knowledge to the task of learning culture. Therefore this learning process involves the child in something akin to hypothesis testing. He or she uses the innate knowledge to build descriptions of the form and content of his or her particular culture and tests those descriptions in action, but not all of these ideas or hypotheses will be correct. Thus the child is bound to make mistakes. Researchers can observe these mistakes as they occur and can use them to reveal the particular culture the child is learning and the body of innate knowledge that the child brings to the task.

Even so, the analogy of the ethnographer to the child must not be carried too far. Their similarity does not go far beyond the fact that both the researcher and the child are learning the culture and often find themselves in subservient roles with respect to the people who are teaching them. Children are almost always subservient to the adults around them; in contrast, researchers interact with the community in many different roles and role structures. Furthermore, the child's social relationships evolve over many years, whereas the field worker's relationships change rapidly (Agar 1980:70–77). The field worker and the child also bring different capacities to the task of learning the culture; the child has an innate universal knowledge base, but the researcher must learn through the filter of his or her home culture.

According to some formulations of the scientific method, qualitative research methods are weak because they lack a means of testing hypotheses. This weakness can be overcome, however, if researchers use error as a means of testing their ideas. Researchers in the field are bound to formulate ideas about what their subjects know and how they use that knowledge. Any explicit proposal about natives' knowledge will imply that certain acts are correct and certain others are in error. Researchers can elicit natives' judgments about incorrect acts, thus providing solid tests of the hypotheses. If the proposal predicts the pattern of error and non-error correctly, the hypothesis is confirmed. If the proposal predicts the pattern incorrectly, the hypothesis is disproved and must be modified. Native judgments regarding error can be elicited either directly or indirectly.

A direct test would involve the performance of an error controlled by the researcher and coupled with observation of native response. The participant observer is the best available research instrument for direct error testing. Field workers are outsiders in the subject community, and they are expected to make mistakes. Thus they enjoy greater freedom of action than the natives and can make mistakes consciously without threatening their standing in the community. This is one advantage to identifying oneself as a researcher in the community rather than conducting the research without the subjects' knowledge.

By the time direct tests are made in the research, the field worker is sensitive to the meaning of natives' responses. He or she has the advantage of having lived for some time with culture shock, which can be turned to the field worker's advantage as a means of learning how natives react to appropriate and inappropriate acts. With greater freedom of action, armed with knowledge of natives' reactions, participant observers can use error to directly test their ideas almost constantly while in the field.

Indirect tests involve natives' reports concerning error. Unlike direct tests, they do not require anyone to make a mistake and can be conducted entirely on a hypothetical level. Either in an interview or in a survey, the researcher asks native consultants how they would react if so-and-so did such-and-such. The information thus acquired, though, is likely to be more idealized than that gained in direct tests.

The most difficult type of error information for researchers to acquire is that generated through errors of purpose made by natives. These errors are subtle; researchers need deep, sophisticated knowledge of the culture to recognize them. In American culture, for example, there is a rule that governs how people behave on sidewalks. If two people are walking on a sidewalk in opposite directions, each will yield to the right to avoid collision. People can violate this rule on purpose for any number of reasons relating to long-term gain, one of which may be to meet the person walking the other way. Researchers alien to the culture would be likely to miss this subtle interaction unless they had a deep understanding of the rules involved. Yet when a field worker has observed and can confirm such an error, it can offer powerful support to his or her ideas.

Data in Ethno-Logic

Ethno-logic is a part of the social sciences, and its goal differs from that of formal philosophical logic. Whereas formal textbook logic seeks to identify how abstract logical systems work, ethno-logic attempts to learn how people think. Human thinking patterns are complex and tacit; they can be described only in terms of intricate interactions between meaning and structure. These interactions take place in the here and now and outside the native actors' awareness. Thus it is impossible through simple introspection to learn how people think and to discover the effect of language and culture on reasoning patterns. Ethno-logicians must collect data using methods that can reveal the knowledge system standing behind their consultants' thought patterns.

The methods of ethno-logical research should be designed to reveal any relationships between meaning and structure that produce a logic. Because validity defines logic, the data should include arguments that do not lead to conclusions, as well as those that do. Furthermore, because language and culture are a part of the logical mix, researchers cannot make a priori judgments about what is valid and what is not. That is, researchers cannot assume that they know what is reasonable in any particular linguistic and cultural setting; the research itself should be used to define validity, from the natives' point of view. Descriptions of intracultural validity can emerge only when the research design considers all possible variations of the particular structure under study. Most ethno-logical research has met these constraints by using the structures defined in logic textbooks, and the most popular structure for this purpose has been the syllogism.

Meaning and Pattern in Syllogisms 4

The previous chapters established the theoretical and methodological background of modern ethno-logic. In this and the two following chapters, I analyze research that I conducted on reasoning patterns. First, I discuss class-inclusion, or syllogistic, reasoning. My data come from four languages: Mende (Mande-Kan), Ojibwa (Algonquian), English (Indo-European), and Navajo (Athabascan). In chapters 5 and 6 I discuss Navajo propositional reasoning.

My methods of studying syllogisms resemble Cole's and Luria's. In each of the four languages I elicited a set of words that were related with "kind of" folk meanings and used these words to generate true premises. Then I combined the premises to produce all possible syllogistic argument patterns and presented these arguments to each consultant. For each argument I asked the consultant to draw a conclusion, noted the response, and later analyzed it.

I elicited this type of syllogistic data from eight consultants over a ten-year period. As mentioned earlier, I conducted some of the research in Milwaukee and the rest at various locations on the central Navajo Indian Reservation near Chinle, Arizona. The consultants ranged in age from five years old (the English speaker) to nearly seventy years old. All were male except one older Navajo. The English speaker and the two older Navajo speakers were monolingual; the rest were bilingual. The Mende speakers and the youngest Navajo consultant were biliterate college students in their mid-twenties. The younger Ojibwa consultant was in his mid-forties and bilingual, but not biliterate.

The results of the syllogism tests were strikingly consistent across the language boundaries. Consultants considered the same kinds of arguments valid and invalid, and in no case did they draw conclusions that were invalid according to the rules of textbook logic. Consultants rejected several arguments that logicians consider valid; all of these involved particular statements for which the corresponding universal statement was true (e.g., "Some oaks are trees"). Thus the natural logic may be more constrained than the logic the textbooks recognize.

These results make sense in light of taxonomic semantics. Responses differed from the textbook syllogistic model in the case of syllogisms containing premises and conclusions that were meaningless according to "kind of" semantics (but not according to textbook logic). Furthermore, because "kind of" meanings are semantic universals, taxonomic semantics account for the similarities between consultants and languages. If meaning structures human reasoning, logical universals will map well to semantic universals.

Methods and Results

The logic found in textbooks on formal reasoning can give us some hints about how to study human reasoning patterns. Yet textbook logic cannot tell us what patterns researchers will find because philosophy studies the properties of logical systems, not human reasoning (Russell 1940). When a logician states that affirming the consequent is a logical fallacy, he or she is referring to a logical system and not to human thinking. The system defines "If A then B" statements in certain truth-functional patterns. The problem in anthropology is to turn these patterns into empirical questions that are open to field research. Textbook logic can set us on the way, but it cannot tell us what the results of the tests will be.

I studied the ethno-logic of class-inclusion reasoning for two reasons. Impressed by a strong tradition of syllogism studies, including the work of Luria, Piaget, and Cole, I hoped to make some contribution to syllogistic research. In addition, cognitive anthropology was maturing, broadening in its scope and interests, and I saw a clear connection between syllogisms and folk classification systems.

Some contemporary ethnosemantic work focuses on the content and formal properties of folk taxonomies (Tyler 1969). Berlin, Breedlove, and Raven (1973) established some structural and morphological universals of folk taxonomies. Brown (1974, 1976a, 1976b) applied those universals in his work on the evolution of taxonomic lexicons. Typically, cognitive anthropologists in ethnosemantics assume that folk taxonomies are a real part of language. They seem to ignore the fact that it is difficult to distinguish between a formal system that research finds in the mind of the native and one that is an artifact of research methods (Burling 1964).

Another area of interest in cognitive anthropology is the representation of native meanings. From this point of view the folk taxonomy is of little interest because it is an overly simplistic representation of human meaning systems. Many semantic features relate words to other words in human meaning systems, only one of which is "kind of" (e.g., an oak is a kind of tree). Further, words are manipulated by many processes (such as reasoning) that formal devices such as folk taxonomies cannot represent. Furthermore, it is difficult, if not impossible, to decide whether a folk taxonomy describes what is in the mind of the consultant or emerges from research procedures. All human languages, however, use "kind of" semantics to relate words to other words, so it is always possible for the research process to filter out all meanings except "kind of" in producing a set of words. It is easy to develop a folk taxonomy from this kind of data, but that taxonomy would not necessarily represent how native speakers actually think about the things mentioned in the data sets.

The problem of representation has two popular solutions in the literature. One proposes a more powerful formal device to replace the taxonomy. Kay (1975), for example, abandoned the set-theoretical basis of taxonomic theory and replaced it with a model-theoretical approach that involved fuzzy sets. When Kempton (1978) tested Kay's ideas, he found that fuzzy set theory did capture significant aspects of how people think, which were opaque to taxonomic theory. The other solution replaces the taxonomy with a formal process. In Werner's solution, Modification, Taxonomy, and Sequence are semantic features that interact with logical, cultural, and linguistic rules as people build the meanings between words. Both of these solutions maintain the universality of "kind of" semantics, which are part of how people think about their world. For my present purposes, the folk taxonomy represents a convenient way to represent part of my data elicitation protocol. I assume that the taxonomy emerged from the interaction between features and rules.

The syllogism is a three-statement argument that deals with class-inclusion relationships. Sometimes the first two sentences in the argument force the third sentence in conclusion; sometimes no conclusion is possible. Four kinds of class-inclusion statements, or propositions (A, E, I, and O), are included in traditional syllogisms:

A All S is P.
E No S is P.
I Some S is P.
O Some S is not P.

The three statements comprising the syllogism are the conclusion, the major premise, and the minor premise. The major premise mentions the predicate term of the conclusion; the minor premise mentions the subject (Barker 1965:61). The terms used in the statements mention classes of objects that either represent kinds of other classes or else include other classes.

Table 4-1
Syllogism Figures

	Figure			
	I	II	III	IV
Major Premise	MS	SM	MS	SM
Minor Premise	RM	RM	MR	MR

Table 4-2
Valid Syllogisms

Mood	Figure			
	I	II	III	IV
AAA	+			
AAI	+		+	+
AEE		+		+
EAE	+	+		
AII	+		+	
IAI			+	+
AOO		+		
OAO			+	
EIO	+	+	+	+
EAO	+	+	+	+
AEO		+		+

Source: Reichenbach 1947:205.

Given that there are four statement (or proposition) types, we have 64 ways to combine statements in groups of three. Logicians call these 64 combinations "moods." The first two statements must "share" one term, called the middle term (M). There are four different ways (called figures) in which the middle term can appear in the first two statements (see table 4-1). Combining figure and mood produces 256 possible syllogisms. A conclusion follows from only 24 of these syllogisms, according to the rules of the logic (see table 4-2). In addition, the major premise (P1) and the minor premise (P2) must mention three terms in all (S, M, and R). P1 mentions S and M, P2 mentions R and M, and the final statement mentions both S and R. All statements must be of the *A, E, I,* or *O* type.

Logicians account for the class of valid syllogisms with a series of rules that define the relationships that must apply among the three statements in order for a conclusion to follow. My methods in this re-

Table 4-3
Lexicon Structure

A			
B		C	
D	E	F	G

Table 4-4
Protocol Sentences

1. All *D* is *B*.	8. No *B* is *C*.	15. Some *D* is not *C*.
2. All *B* is *A*.	9. No *C* is *B*.	16. No *C* is *D*.
3. All *D* is *A*.	10. Some *B* is not *D*.	17. Some *B* is *A*.
4. Some *B* is *D*.	11. Some *A* is not *D*.	18. Some *C* is not *D*.
5. Some *A* is *B*.	12. Some *A* is not *B*.	19. Some *D* is *A*.
6. Some *A* is *D*.	13. Some *B* is not *C*.	20. Some *C* is not *B*.
7. No *D* is *C*.	14. Some *A* is not *C*.	21. Some *D* is *B*.

search included textbook syllogisms and native semantic fields. The fields contained at least seven related words. In each field it was possible to define a path between any two of the words with strictly "kind of" meanings. All of the actual fields that were elicited conformed to the general structure shown in table 4-3.

The words in the semantic fields were used as the M, S, and R terms in sentence frames. The frames corresponded to the *A, E, I,* and *O* sentences in the consultant's language. I used the frames and the field to construct the twenty-one sentences in table 4-4, and I combined these sentences to form all of the sixty-four possible figures and moods in a syllogistic argument (major and minor premises) (see table 4-5, in which the arabic numbers refer to the protocol sentences in table 4-4 and the Xs refer to syllogisms for which there are no valid textbook conclusions).

Once the syllogisms were constructed, the consultants were given each syllogism in their own language and were asked to draw a conclusion. If a consultant drew the textbook-correct conclusion, that response was noted, and then the next syllogism was presented. In some cases, such as the *AA* syllogism of Figure II (listed in table 4-5), no conclusion was the correct response.

Responses could differ from the textbook logic in two ways. Consultants could draw conclusions that did not follow under textbook logic, or they could refuse to draw conclusions that did follow. When

Table 4-5
Protocol Sentence Combinations

	Figure					Figure			
	I	II	III	IV		I	II	III	IV
AA	2	2	1	1	AI	1	1	2	2
	1	3	3	2		6	5	4	6
	3, 19	X	5	6		5	X	19	X
AE	2	1	1	1	AO	3	1	2	2
	9	9	7	8		10	12	10	11
	X	7, 16	X	7, 16		X	11	X	X
IA	6	5	4	6	II	4	4	5	5
	2	1	2	1		5	6	6	4
	X	X	6	17		X	X	X	X
IE	4	5	4	4	IO	4	4	5	5
	9	9	8	7		12	11	11	10
	X	X	X	X		X	X	X	X
EA	8	9	7	9	EI	7	9	8	9
	1	1	1	2		4	5	4	4
	7, 16	7, 16	13	14		13	14	15	15
EE	9	7	9	7	EO	7	9	8	9
	7	8	16	9		10	12	10	10
	X	X	X	X		X	X	X	X
OA	11	12	10	11	OI	10	10	11	12
	2	1	2	1		5	6	5	4
	X	X	11	X		X	X	X	X
OE	10	12	10	10	OO	10	10	11	12
	9	9	8	7		12	11	12	10
	X	X	X	X		X	X	X	X

consultants were able to give a conclusion but did not do so, I asked them whether they agreed with a conclusion I gave. When consultants drew textbook-invalid conclusions, I asked them to argue toward their conclusions and noted what they said.

I varied the semantic fields from language to language to accomplish two purposes (see table 4-6). First, using native semantic fields ensured that the terms of the arguments in the tests would be familiar

Table 4-6
Syllogism Test Categories

M: *huanga* (animal) O: *awasiwag* (living things) E: toys N: *nanisi* (plants)			
M: *besi* (pig) O: *gigoyag* (fish) E: boats N: *tsin* (trees)		M: *nikei* (cattle) O: *bineshiyag* (birds) E: toy cars N: *ch'il* (grasses)	
M: *besi hei* (sow) O: *konoshiway* (pike) E: sailboats N: *gad* (cedar)	M: *besi hini* (boar) O: *nameyag* (sturgeon) E: motor boats N: *t'iss* (cottonwood)	M: *nika hei* (cow) O: *miqizi yag* (bald eagle) E: matchbox racer N: *ch'il diilghesii* (snakeweed)	M: *nika hini* (bull) O: *gokoko'wag* (owl) E: pinewood racer N: *ch'il'abe'e* (milkweed)

Note: M = Mende, O = Ojibwa, E = English, and N = Navajo.

to the consultants and that the premises would be true. Second, using different semantic fields would factor out consultants' possible agreement on logic actually based on agreement about subject matter.

In each of the languages some responses were textbook-correct, and some apparently were not. Overall, consultants drew 16 of the 24 textbook-valid syllogisms. Twelve were drawn in Mende and Ojibwa, 13 in English, and 14 in Navajo. Consultants always rejected at least 40 of the 45 textbook-invalid syllogisms. The English-speaking consultant rejected them all, the Ojibwas rejected 42, the Navajos rejected 42, and the Mende consultants rejected 40. Consultants in each language drew a few conclusions that appeared to be textbook-invalid (8 in Mende, 7 in Ojibwa, 3 in English, and 4 in Navajo). Consultants also rejected several textbook-valid arguments (9 in Mende, 11 in Ojibwa, 7 in English, and 5 in Navajo). I will discuss the textbook-invalid responses first.

One Mende consultant drew three conclusions that could not be drawn under classical syllogistic logic (*EIE*, Figure I; *AEE*, Figure III; and *IEE*, Figure IV). The conclusion in each case was either "No cows are pigs" or its converse, "No pigs are cows." Since no two statements constructed from the semantic field can lead to this conclusion, I reasoned that (1) the consultant could have been using some form of logic of which I was not aware, (2) he could have been reasoning from categories (perhaps covert) that he had not made explicit in the semantic field, or (3) he could have been reasoning from information contained in the words of the premises themselves.

If the consultant was using another logic, he would have drawn analogous conclusions whenever he used the same argument structure that produced "No cows are pigs." To learn whether he was using some other logic, I asked him to draw conclusions from the following argument:

All sows are pigs.
No sows are brown.

If he had concluded "No pigs are brown," I could have assumed that he was using some other inferential rules, but that was not the case. He refused to draw any conclusion, so I tried to discover higher-ranking categories above pigs that excluded cows, as schematized in table 4-7. I asked questions such as "Are horses kinds of cows?" (response: "no") and "What are horses and cows?" (response: "animals"), but I could find no such category, either overt or covert. These responses led to a search for meaning features that *besi* has in Mende but which *nikei* lacks.

I elicited these features by asking questions such as "How are cows and pigs different?" The consultant responded that cows, among other things, were taller than pigs, so a feature of +/− short was proposed, and the consultant was given the following argument:

P1: *Besi sia ti gutango.*	All pigs are short.
P2: *Hei na gbile kutango, nika ya no.*	No thing that is short is a cow.
Conclusion: *Nika nga ya besi sia.*	No cows are pigs.

The consultant responded with, and believed, this conclusion. Therefore I concluded that he had used a feature such as "short" to draw the

Table 4-7
Hypothetical Categories

huanga (animals)			
X		Y	
W	*besi* (pig)	*nikei* (cattle)	Z

conclusions in the original text. In other words, the consultant argued validly using features inherent to the terms. The invalid syllogism in the original test suggests this added feature and is not evidence of some other logic operating.

For several syllogisms all consultants appeared to draw textbook-invalid conclusions. Further investigation of these conclusions revealed that the consultants had changed the premises from which the conclusions had followed. For example, one Mende consultant was given the following *IE*, Figure I argument (see table 4-5): "Some pigs are sows. No cows are pigs." He concluded, "No cows are sows." This response is invalid, but when asked to repeat the argument he said:

All sows are pigs.
No cows are pigs.
Therefore no cows are sows.

He had changed the major premise, and thus the conclusion followed.

In an English test the English-speaking consultant made similar changes in the argument. He was given the *AI*, Figure III argument: "All toy cars are toys. Some toy cars are matchbox racers." He concluded, "Some toys are matchbox racers." When asked to argue toward his conclusion he changed the order of the premises to a valid *IA*, Figure III syllogism.

An Ojibwa-speaking consultant reacted to the *OA*, Figure III syllogism in a similar manner. In response to "Some fish are not pike. All fish are living things" he concluded, "All pike are living things." He changed both the order of the premises and the original major premise to resemble the *AA*, Figure I syllogism as follows: "All fish are living things. All pike are fish."

A Navajo speaker was presented with the *EO*, Figure II syllogism: "No grasses are trees. Some plants are not trees." He gave the conclusion, "Some plants are not grasses." When challenged on this conclusion, he changed the minor premise to "Some plants are trees" and repeated his conclusion, which now followed.

In all of these cases of invalidly drawn conclusions (except the three Mende syllogisms discussed above), similar changes in premises occurred. Furthermore, in all of these instances the change in premises was such that after the change the conclusion followed under textbook logic. Therefore no conclusion was drawn invalidly in any of the tests.

In several cases, consultants rejected apparently valid conclusions. Although these syllogisms were textbook valid, they had conclusions that consultants would neither draw nor accept. In each of these

Table 4-8
Invalidly Rejected Conclusions

Language	Mood	Figure	Conclusion Rejected (Gloss)
Mende	*AII*	I	Some sows are animals
	EIO	I	Some pigs are not cows.
	EAO	I	Some sows are not cows.
	AEO	II	Some cows are not sows.
	EAO	II	Some sows are not cows.
	EAO	III	Some pigs are not cows.
	EIO	III	Some sows are not cows.
	AEO	IV	Some sows are not cows.
	EIO	IV	Some sows are not cows.
English	*AAI*	I	Some matchbox racers are toys.
	EAO	I	Some matchbox racers are not toys.
	EAO	II	Some matchbox racers are not toys.
	AEO	II	Some toy boats are not matchbox racers.
	EAO	III	Some toy cars are not toy boats.
	AEO	IV	Some toy boats are not matchbox racers.
	IAI	IV	Some toy cars are toys.
Ojibwa	*AAI*	I	Some pike are living things.
	EIO	I	Some fish are not birds.
	EAO	I	Some pike are not birds.
	EAO	II	Some pike are not birds.
	AEO	II	Some birds are not pike.
	AII	III	Some pike are living things.
	EAO	III	Some fish are not birds.
	EIO	III	Some pike are not birds.
	IAI	IV	Some fish are living things.
	EIO	IV	Some pike are not birds.
	AEO	IV	Some birds are not pike.
Navajo	*AAI*	I	Some cedars are plants.
	EIO	I	Some trees are not grasses.
	AII	III	Some cedars are plants.
	EIO	III	Some cedars are not grasses.
	EIO	IV	Some cedars are not grasses.

cases the conclusion was a particular statement for which the corresponding universal statement was also true. All of the invalidly rejected conclusions are listed in table 4-8.

These conclusions are interesting because of their similarity of structure and because they constrain the class of drawable conclusions, showing that natural logic is stricter than classical philosophical logic. They also show that descriptions of natural logic can apply across language boundaries. The common view is that natural logic (common sense?) is looser than rigorous self-conscious thought, but it should come as no surprise that a "meaning-filled" structure is more constrained than a similar structure without meaning. Options almost always become more narrow as structures acquire meaning.

Those syllogisms in which consultants drew valid conclusions also suggest universal reasoning structure. In each language, consultants drew 12, 13, or 14 conclusions from the 64. Consultants in all languages drew 10 of the conclusions. Only 2 of the conclusions were limited to a single language (English *EIO*, Figure I, and Navajo *IAI*, Figure IV). The validly rejected conclusions also suggest universal behavior. Consultants validly rejected 40 to 45 conclusions in each of the four languages. In all of the languages 38 conclusions were rejected; each conclusion was rejected in at least three of the four languages.

The responses in the four tested languages exhibit too many common properties to depend either on language or on culture. Essentially, in each of the four languages consultants validly drew or rejected the same set of conclusions. Invalidly drawn conclusions were based on changed premises. Cole's and Luria's consultants exhibited similar behavior. All invalidly rejected conclusions involved particular statements for which the corresponding universal statement was also true.

Furthermore, factors such as bilingualism, schooling, literacy, or acculturation cannot account for these results. Not all of the consultants were bilingual (two Navajo speakers and the English speaker were monolingual). One Ojibwa and two Navajo consultants had received little or no formal education; none of those three could read or write. The consultants also exhibited widely varying degrees of acculturation. The Mende speakers were almost totally acculturated to Western values, the Ojibwa consultants were much less so, and two of the Navajo consultants were almost totally unacculturated. Yet in spite of all of these differences, consultants exhibited almost no variation in their responses to the syllogism tests.

Conclusions

Logicians explain the classes of acceptable and unacceptable syllogisms on the basis of four rules (Barker 1965:69):

> Rule 1: In any valid syllogism, the middle term is extended at least once.
> Rule 2: In any valid syllogism, no term is extended in the conclusion that is not extended in the premises.

Rule 3: No valid syllogism has two negative premises.
Rule 4: Any valid syllogism has one negative premise if and only if it has a negative conclusion.

When applied to all of the possible syllogisms, these rules generate the twenty-four valid forms in table 4-2. These rules, however, are not powerful enough to account for the natural patterns detailed above. They generate too many valid forms, and their explanatory value is weak because they account for nothing other than the syllogism. On the other hand, "kind of" meanings are universal structures within human language. Because taxonomic meanings relate classes of things, they offer an excellent medium to account for the findings.

"Kind of" is a bidirectional semantic structure. In the upward direction Bs are kinds of As (oaks are kinds of trees). In the downward direction As include Bs as kinds. "Kind of" paths from one category to another that include both upward and downward directions produce a horizontal dimension of exclusion. Accordingly, A syllogistic statements ("All B is A") are upward vertical, E statements ("No B is A") are horizontal, and I and O statements ("Some B is A," and "Some B is not A") are downward vertical.

Defining I and O statements as downward vertical accounts for the class of rejected valid conclusions. The meaning of "some" in textbook logic is "there exists," which, in taxonomic semantics, could be interpreted as upward vertical. It is true to say, for example, "There exists a cedar (S) that is a tree (R)." This statement could imply a taxonomic structure like

In "kind of" semantics, however, this R and S would be synonymous and occupy the same node. By defining I and O statements as downward vertical we require a structure like

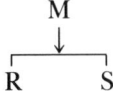

Here R and S are members of a contrast set, neither of which is synonymous with M or with each other. Downward vertical statements like this one are true if and only if their contrapositives are also true under natural logic. In other words, if "Some M is R" is true, "Some M

is not R" must also be true. Thus in the case of valid syllogisms in classical logic that contain premises or conclusions that are both upward vertical and particular, consultants reject valid conclusions. The natural logic consultants use is more constrained than the classical logic.

Taxonomic meanings also explain the class of valid natural syllogisms. No valid syllogism, under classic logic, can contain two premises that are downward vertical; both premises must mention the same class, and at least one premise must mention all members of the class. These principles define the structure of the syllogism and correspond to Rule 1 of classical syllogistic logic, which demands that the middle term be extended at least once. Rule 2 can be expressed as "If the conclusion mentions all members of a node, they must be mentioned in one of the premises." The classical rules mentioning negation (Rules 3 and 4) can be maintained without referring to taxonomic meaning. Noncategorical or propositional reasoning patterns will use negation; the classical rules will serve there.

Viewing the syllogism in terms of taxonomic semantics accounts for the consultants' responses because taxonomic semantics are universal. The results explained above do not demonstrate that syllogistic reasoning is universal; rather they show that people use a common logical base. The syllogism is as much a product of Western culture as is the folk taxonomy, and it does not describe much of what goes on outside academic circles. Nonetheless, these results are valuable, not because all of the consultants were reasoning syllogistically (something we cannot conclude), but because all consultants responded in the same way to syllogistic arguments.

In the case of reasoning patterns that employ nonuniversal meanings, the response patterns that emerge should vary with language and culture. Propositional reasoning offers an opportunity to study this possibility. Research shows that propositional reasoning depends heavily on sentential semantics (Staudenmayer 1975:69–77). Thus, variations in sentential semantics should go along with variations in patterns of propositional reasoning. Assume, for example, that the truth value of "and"-conjoined sentences depends on syntactic time markers in the conjunct sentences. In such a case research results should show different propositional reasoning patterns in different languages. To determine whether meaning structures reasoning, research must detail the patterns that exist. This research then must correlate those patterns to both universal and particular semantic patterns.

Propositional Reasoning and Navajo Subject Pronouns   5

The Navajo language offers an excellent opportunity for ethnological study. It has no tradition of self-conscious textbook logic, and, as an Athabascan language, it is not related to the Indo-European family. Furthermore, Navajo has been largely unaffected by linguistic contact. It contains few loan words, and only recently has it adopted an alphabet to begin a literary tradition.

Navajo culture has persisted and remains a distinct, complete way of life for growing numbers of people (Vogt 1961). This is not to say that today's Navajo is the same as the Navajo of 500 years ago, or 100 or 50 years ago. Rather, the Navajo culture has evolved in Navajo terms. Navajo people have been able to manage and control the contacts between themselves and foreign peoples.

The evolution of Navajo transportation is a typical example of this control. Unlike their predecessors, who as recently as forty years ago still used traditional means of transportation, present-day Navajo commonly own motor vehicles, which they drive on all-weather roads that the Navajo people built. Their word for these vehicles is *chidí*, which means something like "the one that sounds like 'chid.'" This word covers what American English speakers call cars, pickup trucks, vans, and off-road vehicles. *Chidí* is a Navajo concept, not a borrowed word or meaning; it reflects the adaptation of an innovation to fit within a traditional value system. For instance, the placement of family members riding in these vehicles reflects traditional roles. It also expresses the rights associated with ownership and preserves the traditional social structure.

Egalitarian politics reflect important traditional Navajo values that have persisted to the present. This is significant here because reasoning is often applied in political persuasion. Egalitarianism is the politics of consensus; for the Navajo it emphasizes group harmony in decision-making processes. Therefore, Navajo culture contains many social mechanisms that bias interactions toward consensus. In contrast, traditional western European cultural values emphasize the politics of power and encourage adversarial social mechanisms that often lead to institutionalized group polarization. Thus Navajo political values provide a cultural context that significantly contrasts with my own. The Navajo language's Athabascan roots and its position within a culture that lacks a literary tradition but features an egalitarian political tradition convinced me to undertake a study of Navajo propositional reasoning.

Our understanding of humanity requires an understanding of human reasoning. We take as a given that human beings think and that thought patterns allow us to draw valid conclusions. Even so, we do not have a firm understanding of those patterns or of how they work. Therefore ethno-logic must include studies in languages and cultures that are outside western European traditions. Cross-cultural investigations in ethno-logic typically concentrate on syllogisms, or class-inclusion logic, and ignore propositional logics, but obviously a complete understanding of human reasoning will not be available until researchers document the cultural components of propositional reasoning.

In some of my research, I sought to document the role of subject pronouns in Navajo ethno-logic. In this study I concentrated on the arrangement of propositions within arguments; I asked native speakers of Navajo to judge the validity of arguments arranged in a paradigm. I conducted three separate tests, one each for translations of "and," "or," and "if . . . then," which the native consultants had developed. The subject pronouns and the strength of the semantic connection between the premises varied in each entry of the test paradigm. Both types of variance played a role in determining the validity of arguments.

This finding can be understood more completely if it is explained in Navajo terms. The Navajo worldview idealizes order, harmony, and group consensus in political decision making. These Navajo values are realized in many cultural mechanisms, among them certain logical structures, that help produce and maintain group harmony. Thus it is necessary to include political and social factors in determining Navajo logical patterns. The need to do so calls into question theories of reasoning that concentrate on purely structural factors.

The Logic of Syllogisms and Propositions

The difference between syllogistic and propositional reasoning lies in the elements that make up their respective arguments. A syllogistic argument refers to classes of things, as in Argument 1:

A(1)   All trees are plants.
        All oaks are trees.
Conclusion: All oaks are plants.

This argument mentions three classes of things: oaks, trees, and plants. It also states how those classes are related in "kind of" relationships (i.e., an oak is a "kind of" tree).

In contrast, propositional arguments consist of statements that are either true or false (propositions). The propositions are combined with logical operators such as "and," "or," and "if . . . then." Argument 2 is an example of propositional reasoning:

A(2)   I ate lunch and went home.
Therefore: I ate lunch.

The conclusion follows in this case because in English "and"-conjoined molecular propositions (in this case, "I ate lunch and went home") are true only when both atomic propositions (in this case, "I ate lunch" and "I went home") are true.

Syllogistic arguments must mention groups of things. Therefore syllogistic rules do not apply to arguments, such as A(2) above, that do not mention categories. People do not often mention class-inclusion relationships in their speech; disjunction and conjunction and the like play a much more important part in discourse. In other words, most reasoning is propositional. Because the truth of propositions is culture-dependent, an understanding of human logic requires the cross-cultural study of propositional arguments.

Methods and Procedures

Throughout this study it was my goal to come to understand the roles of subject pronouns in Navajo ethno-logic. Thus I asked native speakers of Navajo to judge the validity of certain propositional arguments. I arranged these arguments in paradigms whose entries varied from one another along two dimensions: the subject pronouns differed in each premise sentence, and the premise propositions were either related or unrelated in meaning. I constructed three separate paradigms to test the three propositional conjoiners glossed in English as "and," "or," and "if . . . then." Thus, variation in the responses to the paradigms would result from the conjoiner used. In addition, variation within a paradigm was designed to depend either on the subject pronoun used or on the semantic relatedness of the atomic propositions.

The research was conducted in a school setting on the central reservation. I was present to help develop funding proposals and to provide assistance in a translation project. When the translators and I discovered our mutual interest in the relationship between thought processes and culture, we began to develop this research, and all of the translation team agreed to act as consultants for the study.

Nine Navajo from six chapters acted as consultants. Four of the nine consultants were men; five were women. They ranged in age from their mid-twenties to their late sixties. The consultants were quite well educated by Navajo standards: all were bilingual, most were biliterate, two held college degrees, and only one did not hold a high school diploma.

The Vygotskian notion of decontextualized mediational means (Wertsch 1985:33–40) describes how the consultants dealt with abstract patterns, whether grammatical or logical. The consultants dealt with the patterns as patterns, outside the context of solving problems. Their approach seems to be common among people schooled in Western institutions. It can be seen clearly in Luria's (1971) and Cole's works (especially Scribner and Cole 1981).

If (as I believe) meanings do structure logic, Navajo subjects with a Western educational background would not exhibit the same thinking patterns as would unschooled Navajo. Therefore the results of this research cannot describe traditional Navajo thinking patterns because the consultants were not "traditional" Navajos. Likewise, if the research results described thinking patterns similar to those of native English speakers, they could be attributed to the consultants' school experience. On the other hand, the differences in thinking patterns that the results showed demonstrate a relationship between logical structure and meaning, even if they do not describe Navajo thinking as it was before contact with European culture.

Although methods in ethno-logic are not well established, thus forcing researchers to devise their own methods, researchers are not limited to restrictive traditions. The consultants and I were able to devise methods that revealed their reasoning patterns in significant depth. We tried many different methods in a process of trial and error. During the research we discussed the advantages and disadvantages of each attempt. Through this process we eventually devised ways to obtain the information we wanted.

The first step of the research was paradigm design and construction. Before arriving at the final design, we rejected several possible paradigms. Some were so complicated that we could not extract the information that we sought; others were so simple that the paradigm itself affected the results. Each successive paradigm included a series of propositional arguments. Each of these arguments contained different subject pronouns in the atomic propositions. Because the paradigms were prototypes, however, we paid little attention to the semantic content of the premises. After administering each prototype to one or more consultants, we analyzed the results and discussed the outcome. In this way we determined the general design of the paradigms. We also discovered that closely related atomic propositions did not behave like less closely related ones. For this reason the final paradigms included a dimension of semantic relatedness.

This dimension refers to the meaning of the propositions used. Each final paradigm consisted of two propositions, which were combined to form a major premise, a minor premise, and a conclusion. Native speakers could view these sentences as either related or unrelated. For example, in English, unrelated propositions may be like Propositions 1 and 2, and related propositions may be like Propositions 3 and 4.

Proposition 1: I am at my desk.
Proposition 2: My car has a flat tire.
Proposition 3: I can read.
Proposition 4: I can write.

The effect of related and unrelated premises on Navajo reasoning patterns was tested by presenting each argument structure in the final paradigm twice; once with related premises and once with unrelated premises.

The atomic sentences that constitute the test paradigms were constructed through discussion. Each of the final tests employed two pairs of sentences: one pair was connected conceptually, while the other was not. Discussion with consultants determined the presence or absence of this conceptual link. We discussed pairs of sentences until we found six appropriate pairs. We needed two pairs for each conjoiner in the final paradigm, one pair linked conceptually and the other pair not so linked. These sentences, along with glosses, are listed in table 5-1.

Many of the sentence pairs in Table 5-1 violate my notions about semantic relatedness. In my terms, for instance, climbing a mountain would make me tired. The object of the study, however, was to describe the consultants' own logical patterns. Thus the test items had to express the consultants' view. Accordingly we used pairs of sentences that the consultants agreed displayed strong semantic relatedness or no relatedness.

We chose the three Navajo conjoiners noted above because they

Table 5-1
Navajo Test Propositions

Conjoiner	Semantic Relationship	Sentence A	Sentence B
áádóó "and"	related	shiłbeez "I cooked it"	yiyáá "I ate it"
	unrelated	na'niłkaad "I am tired"	adełt'i' "I am sleepy"
éédoodaii' "or"	related	nisneez "I am tall"	insiłt'isí "I am short"
	unrelated	hogangóó nidietsa "I will go home"	kingóó deeshoot "I will go to the store"
diégó "if . . . then"	related	yiiłtam "I see him"	bithweeshne' "I will tell him"
	unrelated	dził baah "I climb the mountain"	ch'ééh déya "I will be tired"

seemed to be significant in Navajo reasoning. In the initial phases of building the test paradigms, we tried to discern something about the consultants' styles of reasoning. In our discussions, "and" and "or" arguments occurred frequently. Conditional patterns (if . . . then), although less prevalent, were crucial in many instances. Therefore the Navajo analogues of "and," "or," and "if . . . then" were elicited through translations of compound sentences. Consultants were not asked to translate "and"; instead they were asked to translate "Johnny went to the store and bought a pair of boots." In their translations, the consultants used several candidate conjoiners, which were discussed until everyone agreed on the most appropriate one. The three conjoiners used in the final paradigm are áádóó (glossed as "and"), éédoodaii', and diégó. Éédoodaii', formed from doo-(verb)-da ("no" or "not") and -ii' ("and"), is glossed as "or." Diégó, perhaps formed from di- (a form that refers to interception of slopes, as a hill with level ground, or two people, as in "come hither") and -go (a durative complimentizer, "when"), is glossed as "if . . . then." The final conjoiner, ako (glossed as "therefore"), appears in all three test paradigms and functions to connect premise to conclusion.

The final elements of the test paradigms were the subject pronouns used in the propositions. Navajo has two sets of subject pronouns that are related morphophonemically but are distinct syntactically. One set includes free-standing morphemes, any one of which is optional in any Navajo sentence. The other set consists of bound morphemes, which are affixed to the verb stem in Position VIII in the Young and Morgan (1980:107) analysis or Position 12 in the Hoijer (1945:196) analysis. These pronouns are obligatory; every Navajo sentence must include one from this set.

Navajo has syntactic rules that govern the use of these pronouns. The obligatory pronoun must agree in person and number with the underlying optional pronoun that may be deleted by late syntactic rules. Therefore, to keep the propositions as simple as possible, we used only the obligatory pronouns in the test paradigm. The underlying forms of the complete set of obligatory pronouns used are listed in table 5-2.

The final test consisted of three subparadigms, one each for the Navajo translations of sentences "*A* and *B*," "*A* or *B*," and "if *A* then *B*." (*A* and *B* refer to the propositions listed in table 5-1.) The paradigms for "or" and "if . . . then" used the same structure: they contained a single major premise, which conjoined two propositions, and a group of eight minor premise/conclusion pairs. This structure represents all of the possible combinations and orders of the propositions stated both positively and negatively (see table 5-3). All paradigms ex-

Table 5-2
Navajo Obligatory Subject Pronouns

Pronoun	Gloss	Syntactic Function
-*shi*-	I	first person singular
-*ni*-	you	second person singular
-θ-	he, she, it	third person singular
-'*ee*-	we two	first person duoplural
-'*o*-	you two	second person duoplural

Table 5-3
"Or," "If . . . Then" Test Design

Major Premise	*A* (or, if . . . then) *B*							
Minor Premise	*A*	*A*	−*A*	−*A*	*B*	*B*	−*B*	−*B*
Therefore	*B*	−*B*	*B*	−*B*	*A*	−*A*	*A*	−*A*

Table 5-4
"And" Test Design

Major Premise	A	A	−A	−A	B	B	−B	−B
Minor Premise	B	−B	B	−B	A	−A	A	−A
Therefore	A and B							

press negation with *doo-da*, a split morpheme glossed as "no" or "not"; *doo* precedes the verb and *da* follows it in the Navajo sentence.

The test paradigm for "and" grouped the propositions into eight major premise/minor premise pairs with a single conclusion (see table 5-4). The "and" test differs from the "or" and the "if . . . then" tests because simple "and" arguments differ from simple arguments employing the other two conjoiners. In "or" and "if . . . then" arguments, a structure similar to that in Argument 3 is common.

    A(3)   A or B   major premise
                      not B   minor premise
    Therefore   A   conclusion

Here the major premise is a molecular proposition made up of two atomic propositions. The minor premise and the conclusion are atomic propositions. Simply to translate this structure into an "and" argument would produce Argument 4.

    A(4)   A and B major premise
                      not A   minor premise
    Therefore   B   conclusion

This argument makes little sense on paper and even less in oral elicitation. The paradigm structure shown in table 5-4, however, is a good representation of simple conjunctive arguments.

Thirty argument sets made up the final test paradigm. There was one argument set for each of the three conjoiners. These three sets varied along two dimensions of semantic relatedness and five dimensions of subject pronouns, thus resulting in a total of thirty individual sets ($3 \times 2 \times 5 = 30$). I presented each of the argument sets in each of the eight possible combinations shown in tables 5-3 and 5-4. This step resulted in a final master paradigm that was 240 arguments long. Next I gave consultants entire arguments consisting of major premise, minor premise, and conclusion. For each argument I asked whether the conclusion was always true, always false, or sometimes true on the basis of the premises. No consultant ever opted for the "sometimes true" choice. A minimum of four consultants and a maximum of eight judged each argument independently.

Three consultants representing at least two Navajo chapters had to agree on any judgment before it was accepted. We placed this constraint on the test before applying it in order to reduce any noise in the data that might have resulted from dialect variation. Although dialect variation occurred in word usage and pronunciation, there was no such variability in the consultants' judgment of validity. Each consultant, when presented with an argument, agreed on its validity with each of the other consultants who judged that argument. This result suggests that although considerable dialect variation exists in Navajo phonology and syntax, there may be almost none in Navajo ethnologic. If this is so, the parameters of Navajo ethno-logic may underlie Navajo culture. In other words, the way a Navajo thinks may define what it means to be a Navajo.

Results

The patterns of responses show that both the semantic relatedness of the premises and the subject pronoun affect the logical patterns. These two factors, however, have different effects in the case of different conjoiners. When the conjoiner was *áádóó* ("and"), neither semantic relatedness nor subject pronoun had any effect. When the conjoiner was *diégó* ("if . . . then"), only semantic relatedness was a factor. When the conjoiner was *éédoodaii'* ("or"), both relatedness and subject pronoun affected the logics displayed.

The responses to the arguments in the *áádóó* paradigm showed no variation with regard either to the relatedness of the atomic premises or to the subject pronoun employed. Throughout the paradigm the conclusion "*A áádóó B*" was true only when both propositions were true and were stated positively in the premises. Otherwise the conclusion was always false. Table 5-5 illustrates the responses to the *áádóó* paradigm test.

If one interprets these results truth-functionally, they show a strict conjunctive logic (Barker 1965:104). The fact that *áádóó* behaves as we would expect it to in Western symbolic logic does not speak to the issue of meaning and reasoning. Even so, it does not rule out the possibility that both conjunction and negation may be common features in both logical systems.

The semantic relatedness of the atomic sentences affects Navajo conditional reasoning. This effect is clearly illustrated by the responses elicited from the *diégó* ("if . . . then") paradigm. "Right" (as opposed to "left") logic resulted when the atomic sentences showed strong seman-

Table 5-5
Áádóó ("And") Test Results

Major Premise			A	A	−A	−A	B	B	−B	−B
Minor Premise			B	−B	B	−B	A	−A	A	−A
Therefore			\multicolumn{8}{c}{A áádóó B}								
Tests	Logics	Subject Pronouns	\multicolumn{8}{c}{Results}								
Related	"and"	-shi-	+	−	−	−	+	−	−	−
		-ni-	+	−	−	−	+	−	−	−
		-θ-	+	−	−	−	+	−	−	−
		-'ee-	+	−	−	−	+	−	−	−
		-'o-	+	−	−	−	+	−	−	−
Unrelated	"and"	-shi-	+	−	−	−	+	−	−	−
		-ni-	+	−	−	−	+	−	−	−
		-θ-	+	−	−	−	+	−	−	−
		-'ee-	+	−	−	−	+	−	−	−
		-'o-	+	−	−	−	+	−	−	−

Note: "+" means that consultants accepted the conclusion as validly drawn, and "−" means that they rejected it.

tic connection. In right logic, the rightmost atomic sentence in the major premise compound controlled the truth of the entire compound and the validity of the entire argument.

A "biconditional" logic appeared when the atomic sentences were not semantically related. In biconditional logic, the entire major premise compound is true only when both of the component sentences are either true or false. Logic texts normally represent the biconditional operation as "if and only if." The differences between right and biconditional responses are shown in table 5-6.

Staudenmayer (1975) found similar results in his study of conditional reasoning among English-speaking college students. His respondents used biconditional logic in "if . . . then"−conjoined sentences in which the atomic propositions were not semantically connected (e.g., "If she waters the plant, then the lights will go on"). On the other hand, conditional logic was exhibited in "if . . . then"–conjoined sentences in which the atomic propositions were semantically connected (e.g., "If I turn the switch, the light will go on"). Thus the semantic relatedness of conditional sentences seems to affect reasoning patterns in both Navajo and English.

The "or" test paradigms produced the most interesting results. In these tests both the subject pronoun and the relatedness of the atomic proposition affected the reasoning patterns. Disjunctive Navajo arguments with semantically related premises displayed "exclusive" logic; that is, the major premise was true only when one or the other of the atomic propositions was true, but not both. When the premises displayed no semantic relationship, the consultants inter-

Table 5-6
Diégó ("If . . . Then") Test Results

Major Premise			A *diégó* B							
Minor Premise			A	A	−A	−A	B	B	−B	−B
Therefore			B	−B	B	−B	A	−A	A	−A
Tests	Logics	Subject Pronouns	Results							
Related	"right"	-*shi*-	+	−	−	+	−	+	+	+
		-*ni*-	+	−	−	+	−	+	+	+
		-*θ*-	+	−	−	+	−	+	+	+
		-'*ee*-	+	−	−	+	−	+	+	+
		-'*o*-	+	−	−	+	−	+	+	+
Unrelated	"biconditional"	-*shi*-	+	−	−	+	+	−	−	+
		-*ni*-	+	−	−	+	+	−	−	+
		-*θ*-	+	−	−	+	+	−	−	+
		-'*ee*-	+	−	−	+	+	−	−	+
		-'*o*-	+	−	−	+	+	−	−	+

Table 5-7
Éédoodaii' ("Or") Test Results

Major Premise			A éédoodaii' B							
Minor Premise			A	A	−A	−A	B	B	−B	−B
Therefore			B	−B	B	−B	A	−A	A	−A

Tests	Logics	Subject Pronouns	Results							
Related	"exclusive disjunction"	-shi-	−	+	+	−	−	+	+	−
		-ni-	Rejected major premise							
		-θ-	−	+	+	−	−	+	+	−
		-'ee-	−	+	+	−	−	+	+	−
		-'o-	Rejected major premise							
Unrelated	"inclusive disjunction"	-shi-	+	+	+	−	+	+	+	−
		-ni-	Rejected major premise							
		-θ-	+	+	+	−	+	+	+	−
		-'ee-	+	+	+	−	+	+	+	−
		-'o-	Rejected major premise							

preted disjunctive arguments inclusively; that is, the entire major premise compound was true when either or both of the atomic propositions were true. In addition, the consultants rejected second-person major premises in both the related and the unrelated tests. All of the consultants agreed that one could say, "You went to the store" and "You went home." One also could say, "I went to the store or I went home." On the other hand, one could not say, "You went to the store or you went home." That statement had to be expressed as a question: "Did you go to the store or go home?" These results are shown in table 5-7.

The "or" tests demonstrate processes at work in Navajo ethnologic similar to those apparent in the "if . . . then" test. No conditional logic appears in the results. Related and unrelated propositions exhibit different logical behavior, and second-person disjunctive arguments are not allowed. These results show that the internal semantics of the sentences contributed to the logical behavior of the arguments. If these results cannot be explained on linguistic grounds alone, then cultural values shared by the consultants must be taken into account.

Accounting for the findings in linguistic terms would be difficult and problematic. For instance, in the case of the second-person data, a linguistic explanation would have to account for the behavior of disjunctive arguments in the syntax of the language; that is, one would have to argue that the language's syntactic rules allowed the following sentences:

(1) *Nisneez.* (I am tall).
(2) *Insitł'isi.* (I am short.)
(3) *Ninineez.* (You are tall.)
(4) *Initł'isi.* (You are short.)
(5) *Nisneez éédoodaii' insitł'isi.* (I am tall, or I am short.)

Those rules, however, would have to block the formation of sentence (6):

(6) *Ninineez éédoodaii' initł'isi.* (You are tall, or you are short.)

In addition, the syntactic rules would have to allow sentence (6) to be expressed as a question. The proposed rules would be ad hoc and would lack any independent motivation in the rest of the language.

The well-known difficulty of eliciting second-person linguistic data does not account for the behavior of these disjunctive arguments, either. If these results originated in an elicitation problem with the second person and not disjunction, then the consultants should have had difficulty with the conditional tests, the conjunction tests, or both. The consultants, however, had no trouble at all responding to "You cooked it, and you ate it" and "If you see him, then you will tell him." Neither linguistic nor methodological considerations account for these data—Navajo cultural values do.

Many anthropologists have documented a heavy emphasis on order in the Navajo worldview. Kluckhohn and Leighton (1962:304) list the maintenance of "orderliness in those sections of life which are little subject to human control" as one of the five principal formulas that Navajo people follow to ensure their safety. According to Witherspoon (1977:25), the goal of Navajo life is to "live to maturity in the condition described as *hózhǫ́*"—that is, in an environment of order, harmony, and beauty. Witherspoon goes on to identify *bik'eh* ("by its decree") *hózhǫ́* as one of the two "central animating powers of the universe." This high value on order expresses itself in social interaction as well as in beliefs about the nature of things.

In the Navajo world, assertion of both order and disorder creates these conditions. Remember that the consultants had three choices with respect to each argument: the conclusion could be true, false, or sometimes true and sometimes false. To assert the third choice would have been to make disorder, to the degree that the consultants participate in this worldview. In order for the data to display conditional reasoning, however, consultants had to make the third choice in some cases.

Conditional reasoning is not very orderly. Under the major premise "If you shovel the snow from my walk, then I will give you five dollars," almost anything can happen without violating the truth—for if you do not shovel my walk and I give you five dollars anyway, the premise is still true and thus I have told the truth. If you do shovel my walk and I give you five dollars, I have also told the truth. I have lied only in the case where you shovel my walk and I do not pay up. Thus conditional reasoning could not appear as a test result without the consultants asserting that certain conclusions were sometimes true and sometimes false. In other words, conditional reasoning violates a fundamental Navajo value. Therefore it was avoided, and the "if . . . then" tests showed either a biconditional logic or a logic that affirmed the truth of the second conjunct in the major premise.

The "if . . . then" tests could not exhibit a conditional pattern because that in itself would produce disorderly ambiguity. An analogy with Western science may help in understanding this phenomenon. The analogy is apt in that science also places a high value on order; there can be no science without an underlying belief in order. The analogy breaks down, however, because science can only discover, whereas *hózhǫ́* can be, and is, made. Thus science is limited to understanding those phenomena that are orderly, but *hózhǫ́* applies productively to all aspects of Navajo life. It provides structure to the cosmos (Farella 1984; McNeley 1981; Reichard 1950), definition to aesthetic values (Witherspoon 1977), and meaning to space (Pinxten, van Dooren, and Harvey 1983).

From time to time we change our views about the structure of scientific arguments. The positivists saw science as hypothesis testing and identified disconfirmability as one of the essential features of theory (Hempel 1965). Kuhn (1962) noted that disconfirming evidence seldom leads to rejection of a theory, and he looked for other conditions to account for the paradigm shifts that occur in science. Recently some philosophers have begun to conceptualize the scientific endeavor as a question-and-answer process: the scientist asks questions and arranges nature in order to find an answer (Laudan 1986). In any case, the hypotheses, paradigms, or questions are representations of underlying regularities that are not easily apparent. That is, all formulations of science require a logical relationship between evidence and idea.

The general structure of scientific argument is conditional. If hypothesis (or paradigm or question) A represents an underlying reality, then the world will be like B. If B turns out not to be true, then hypothesis A is not true, and either A is changed, or else B is put into some sort of exceptions bin. If B is true, ironically, the scientist cannot conclude that A is true because in this case A can be either true or false. The first part of this structure is analogous to the related-premise *diégó* ("if . . . then") results: to the consultants (as to the scientist) the A statement could not be true if the B statement were false. Unlike the scientist, however, these consultants would not agree that the truth of A would be indeterminate in the case that B were true. This view produces the "right" logic in the results.

In some cases scientists find it difficult or impossible to make a direct test of a relationship between A and B, so they test the idea that there is no relationship. In this case, when a true A produces a false B or a false A produces a true B, the relationship that the major premise asserts is false. When a true A creates a true B and a false A creates a false B, then there is a good chance that a relationship exists between A and B. This is the biconditional logic that the unrelated *diégó* results exhibit.

The logical differences between semantically related and unrelated *éédoodaii'* ("or")-conjoined sentences also can be understood as an expression of the high value placed on order and harmony. Semantically related "or" compounds exhibit exclusive disjunction in which both atomic propositions could not be true at the same time. To assert that an "or"-conjoined compound is true when both semantically related conjuncts are true is to assert either that the relationship is false or that the disjunction is false. Such a statement would assert, and therefore produce, disharmony. This principle does not apply to unrelated conjuncts; in such cases inclusive disjunction is the result.

The absence of second-person disjunction also is a derivative of the Navajo value on harmony and order. In social terms the Navajo is both an individual and a member of a group. Thus Navajo people live in a dilemma: their values require a high degree of individualism but at the same time demand smooth, harmonious relationships with others (Reichard 1950:xxxviii). Ideally a Navajo arrives at a conclusion and follows it through with little concern for others' plans and goals. This ideal is reinforced by the ceremonial privilege of lying three times when presented with a question. At the fourth asking one should tell the truth (Reichard 1950:131). Navajo people balance this individualism in part by placing a high value on harmony and order. One's decision may be "talked down" in the political context of the family or the local group, but the talking down should always take the form of gentle persuasion, relying heavily on circumstantial evidence (Reichard 1950:131) and should never employ high-pressure tactics (Reichard 1950:xlix). The Navajo people resolve the conflict between self and group with an egalitarian political system that operates on the basis of consensus (Gorman 1973:19–22) and follows from the high value placed on order.

The Navajo ideal is for all to agree and to reach consensus, but the Navajo do not occupy some moral or behavioral high ground with respect to other peoples. They are just as good and bad, just as contentious and courteous, and just as considerate and selfish as everybody else. The various aspects of Navajo culture are also like other peoples' in that they are simultaneously expressions of values and mechanisms for living up to those values. I believe that the consultants treated second-person disjunction as one cultural means of avoiding rhetorical styles that polarize the group. Disjunctive reasoning can lead only to polarization because it asserts opposition ("A or B"). If that opposition is applied to self (first-person) or to someone other than the hearer (third-person), the polarization need not apply to the group. If it is applied to the hearer (second-person), however, it will divide the group. To assert "You are A or you are B" leaves hearers with very little room to move. They must choose one side or the other and thus assert a split in the group, or they must deny the disjunction that divides one from the speaker.

The most striking finding from the research was that second-person disjunctives—*ni* ("you") and *o* ("you" duoplural)—could not be expressed as statements, but had to be phrased as questions. This constraint does not arise from either the syntax or the semantics of the language. Either conjunct sentence can be expressed grammatically as a statement, and the entire compound can be expressed as a statement if the subject pronoun is not in second-person or if the conjoiner is not *éédoodaii'*. Rather, the constraint arises from the etiquette of argumentation, which I contend is a derivation of consensus politics. A similar phenomenon occurs in some Anglo-American institutions that value egalitarian ideals. Parliamentary rules of order usually assume that the members are equals and dictate that they refer to one another in the third-person.

In general these results show that both the semantics of the atomic proposition and the subject pronoun employed have an effect

Propositional Reasoning and Subject Pronouns 89

on the reasoning patterns displayed in Navajo ethno-logic. More interestingly, the results cannot be understood on strictly linguistic grounds. If we consider only the syntax and the semantics of the language, we cannot account for many of the logical transformations. Yet if we allow for the broader issues of Navajo values in the equation, the results are opened to clear interpretation. The same is true of the interaction of syntactic time markers with Navajo reasoning patterns.

Propositional Reasoning and Navajo Syntactic Time 6

Validity makes logic seem secure. A valid logical form leads to a conclusion with every use. Form, however, is only one aspect of validity; there is also semantic validity. Where meanings define validity, similar semantic structures will produce similar logical patterns and dissimilar semantic structures will produce dissimilar logical patterns. Syllogisms are valid reasoning forms worldwide because the "kind of" relationship is a semantic universal. It is beside the point that the "kind of" relationship may be an aspect of perception for any being able to perceive and may not exclusively apply to human beings; the "kind of" meaning certainly is universal among people, no matter what its wider application. In contrast, validity in the case of universal propositional reasoning is not as strong an example. Propositional logics depend heavily on the internal semantics of their premises, and these clearly are not universal.

In the field season of 1979 I studied the effects of syntactic time (e.g., past and present in English) on Navajo propositional reasoning. I chose time as the semantic focus of the study because all human language sentences express time. Thus comparative studies in other natural languages would be possible.

Navajo Compound Sentences

Propositional logic is expressed in truth conditions that make compound declarative sentences true. The compound sentences consist of declarative sentences that are put together with conjoiners. These conjoiners are the logical operators; they code the logic. Thus any description of the effects of syntactic time on truth functions of Navajo conjoiners must meet at least three conditions. It must identify the conjoiners and the syntactic time markers being used; it must describe the truth-functional logic of each compound sentence; and it must enumerate the principles that stand behind the entire system. The methods that I developed to satisfy these conditions involved two separate procedures. The first determined the Navajo time markers that can be conjoined with one another in compound sentences. The second determined the logic that those correct molecular sentences exhibit.

In the subject pronoun study the conjoiners were the nearest possible Navajo translations of "and," "or," and "if . . . then." Thus, to some extent, the study imposed western European values on Navajo data. In this study I chose conjoiners on linguistic grounds; I investigated four Navajo sentential conjoiners that could not function in adverbial or other syntactic roles (see table 6-1.) The Navajo language expresses syntactic time in nine modes or aspects and in a future tense. The modes express the action of the verb along various semantic dimensions such as completeness (is the action complete?) and iteration (does the action recur, and how?). These time markers are given in table 6-2.

I elicited a master paradigm that represented an exhaustive list of all possible time-signature pairs in Navajo compounds. This para-

Table 6-1
Navajo Sentential Conjoiners

Conjoiner	Gloss
biniinaa	because of it
áádóó	and from there on
dóó	and
éédoodaii'	or

Table 6-2
Navajo Time Markers

Time Markers	Gloss
Neuter aspect	states quality
Future tense	verb action in the future
Imperfect mode	verb action is incomplete
Yi Perfect mode	action just completed
Ni Perfect mode	action complete, resulting in a static condition
Si Perfect mode	completed durative act
Progressive mode	verb action in progress
Usitative mode	verb action habitual
Iterative mode	verb action repeats
Optive mode	verb action potential

digm consisted of all the compound sentences for which I collected truth functions. It included four paradigms, one for each conjoiner tested. Each paradigm in turn was made up of ten subparadigms, one for each of the Navajo time signatures tested. Each sentence in the master paradigm had the following structure:

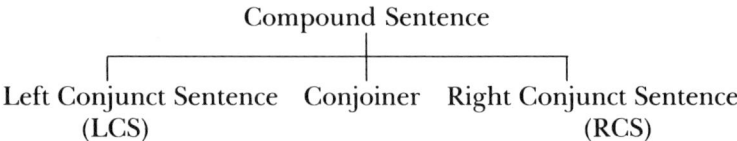

This structure produces a master paradigm that is a maximum of 400 sentences long (10 LCS time signatures × 10 RCS time signatures × 4 conjoiners). Yet because no Navajo verb stem is conjugated in all time signatures, the RCS entries in any one paradigm did not include all ten entries. Therefore the actual paradigm size was much smaller. A verb stem, subject pronouns, object pronouns (where appropriate), and a time signature made up the conjunct sentences. To keep them as simple as possible I included no nouns, adjectives, or adverbs. For example, the left conjunct sentence in the *yi*-perfective mode is *yinizh* ("I plucked it").

The subparadigms consisted of sentences that held the LCS time signature and the conjoiner constant while varying the RCS time signature. In the subparadigm, the RCS entries displayed all of the time signatures in which the particular root verb was conjugated. I elicited judgments as to grammaticality for each LCS-RCS pair in the case of each conjoiner. Because the semantics of the conjunct sentences were constant, variations in the pattern of good or bad sentences could be traced exclusively to the conjoiner. Each subparadigm in the master contained grammatically acceptable sentences, and no subparadigm was ungrammatical in all conjoiners. Therefore the lack of semantic richness in the conjunct sentences did not contribute to the grammaticality of the compound sentences.

In the first step of data collection I recorded the master paradigm on audiotape. Then I played back the tape to Navajo consultants and asked them to judge the grammaticality of the entries in the paradigm. I consulted a total of ten speakers of Navajo ranging in age from twenty-one to sixty-five years. Three of the ten were bilingual in Navajo and English; the remainder were monolingual in Navajo. Two of the consultants judged the entire paradigm; no consultant judged any fewer than two of the subparadigms. Judgments from no fewer than four reliable consultants were elicited for each of the subparadigms. I ignored the judgments of two consultants. One responded that each of the entries was bad; this consultant believed that I was a witch trying to steal the Navajo language, and therefore she did not wish to cooperate. The other responded that all entries were good. I felt that these responses were equally unreliable and therefore I ignored them.

This procedure produced a list of fifty-nine acceptable conjunctions of Navajo time. Absent from the final list were any compounds that expressed the optative, neuter, and progressive modes. All of the reliable consultants said that they had never heard or used language expressing those times. Therefore, the sentences included here provide an adequate basis for investigating the effects of syntactic time markers on Navajo ethno-logic.

I elicited data in the logic test by asking consultants whether the whole compound sentence was true or false for each of the four true/false combinations of the left and right conjunct sentences. I used five consultants, ranging in age from twenty-one to forty years old, for this part of the research, and I asked each consultant to judge all sentences.

Syntactic Time in Navajo Ethno-Logic

I used procedures laid down by Quine (1960:57–58) to determine the logic of Navajo propositional reasoning. Quine defines "radical translation" as the "translation of the language of hitherto untouched people." Although no one can describe the Navajo as untouched, the problem of translating Navajo logical conjoiners is radical in Quine's terms.

In order to translate logical conjoiners, Quine proposes the use of truth functions. In his method, researchers present native speakers with compound sentences. Then they ask consultants to assent or dissent to the truth of the entire compound for each of the truth conditions of the component sentences (Quine 1960:57–58). In the translation of English "and," for example, a researcher would find a native speaker of English and give him or her a sentence like (1):

(1) Johnny went to the store and bought a pair of shoes.

The researcher then would ask the native speaker whether the entirety of (1) was true or false in four separate cases. The first case would be that Johnny both went to the store and bought a pair of shoes. The second case would be that Johnny went to the store but did not buy a pair of shoes. In the third case Johnny did not go to the store but did buy a pair of shoes; in the fourth case Johnny neither went to the store nor bought a pair of shoes. Let us imagine further that our

Table 6-3
"Radical" Translation of English "And"

A	B	A and B
T	T	T
T	F	F
F	T	F
F	F	F

A = Johnny went to the store.
B = Johnny bought a pair of shoes.

Table 6-4
Logics Exhibited by Navajo Conjoiners

p	q	"and"	"or"	"left"	"right"
1	2	3	4	5	6
T	T	T	T	T	T
T	F	F	T	T	F
F	T	F	T	F	T
F	F	F	F	F	F

native speaker judged the first case true but said that the others were false. Those responses are shown in table 6-3.

This translation of English "and" is the logical "and" that one may find in a logic text. Logical "and," however, has little relationship to the way "and" is used in English. Natural language conjoiners such as "and" and "if . . . then" display logics that vary according to semantic conditions in the conjunct sentences (Staudenmayer 1975:73–75).

The Navajo data exhibited four logics. "And" logic (see table 6-3) emerged in some sentences. "Or" logic, in which the sentence is true if either conjunct is true, also appeared. The other two logics affirmed one of the conjuncts in the compound sentence. In "left affirmative" logic, the sentence is true if the left, or first, conjunct sentence is true. In "right affirmative" logic, the right, or second, conjunct governs the truth of the entire compound. These four logics are shown in table 6-4.

Western Europeans recognize the "and" and "or" logics, but the "left" and "right" logics may appear deviant to them. Yet both of these logics can be derived from the assumptions of the propositional calculus. Therefore they are theorems of the calculus and are internally consistent. The logics of all the conjoiners varied with the times expressed in the conjunct sentences. In each conjoiner, however, the logic was consistent in the perfective modes. The logic was also consistent in the future tense, usitative, and iterative modes. Therefore I collapsed the three perfective modes into a single perfective category and collapsed the future tense, iterative, and usitative modes into a single iterative category.

Two of the conjoiners exhibited two logics dependent on the time configuration of the conjunct sentences. The logic of *biniinaa* was "and" in all time pairs that did not express one of the iterative categories; otherwise, it was "left." Thus sentence (2) is true only if both conjuncts are true, and sentence (3) is true only if the leftmost conjunct is true.

(2) *Néljool   biniinaa   diniiltl'iizh.*
    I rolled it | *biniinaa* | I soaked it.

(3) *Deeshcha   biniinaa   hodishne'.*
    I will cry | *biniinaa* | I will tell.

When the LCS is in one of the perfective modes, *éédoodaii'* exhibits "right" logic, and *éédoodaii'* also exhibits "right" logic in the LCS iterative/RCS iterative pair. In other time configurations, however, it shows "left" logic. Thus sentence (4) is true if the left conjunct is true, but sentence (5) is true only when the right conjunct is true.

(4) *Nishteeh   éédoodaii'   'iideeshhoch.*
    I lay | *éédoodaii'* | I will sleep.

(5) *Yinizh   éédoodaii'   yishghal.*
    I plucked it | *éédoodaii'* | I am eating (meat).

Each of the remaining conjoiners tested—*áádóó* and *dóó*—exhibits three logics in various time configurations. The logic of *áádóó* is "right" when the LCS is in one of the perfective modes. It is "and" when both the RCS and the LCS are imperfect, and it is "left" elsewhere. Thus sentence (6) is true when the right conjunct sentence is true; sentence (7) is true only when both conjuncts are true; and sentence (8) is true when the left conjunct is true.

(6) *Séziigo   áádóó   disets'áá'.*
    I stood | *áádóó* | I heard it.

(7) *Nishteeh   áádóó   'iishhaash.*
    I lay | *áádóó* | I am sleeping.

(8) *Nishteeh   áádóó   'iideeshhosh.*
    I lay | *áádóó* | I will sleep.

Table 6-5
The Logic of Navajo Conjoiners
with Respect to Syntactic Time Markers

Logic	Time Category (LCS/RCS)					
	PRF/PRF	PRF/IMP	PRF/ITR	IMP/IMP	IMP/ITR	ITR/ITR
"and"	bini	bini		áádóó		
"or"			dóo			
"left"		dóó	bini	dóó édo	dóó édo áádóó	
"right"	áádóó dóó	áádóó	áádóó			édo

Note: bini = biniinaa; édo = éédoodaii'.

The conjoiner *dóó* is usually translated "and" both in the literature and by bilingual Navajos. In no cases, however, did *dóó* exhibit "and" logic. When either the LCS or the RCS expresses the imperfect mode, its logic is "left." It is "right" in LCS perfective/RCS perfective pairs, and it is "or" elsewhere. Thus sentence (9) is true when the left conjunct is true; sentence (10) is true only when the right conjunct is true; and sentence (11) is true if either conjunct is true.

(9) *Yinizh   dóó   yishghal.*
    I plucked it | *dóó* | I am eating (meat).

(10) *Séziigo   dóó   diséts'áá'*
     I stood | *dóó* | I am hearing it.

(11) *Séziigo   dóó   dideests'iil.*
     I stood | *dóó* | I will hear it.

Table 6-5 summarizes the logics of the conjoiners found in each of the time category groupings. These results are startling. Although I expected variations in logic with respect to time, both the kind of logical changes and their distribution were surprising. I was prepared to find "and" and "or" logic, and I hoped to see some conditional ("if . . . then") patterns emerging. The appearance of the "left" and "right" modes was a surprise. I also believed that "and" and "or" logics would dominate Navajo patterns. Yet only three of ten time marker/conjoiner/time marker triads in table 6-5 exhibit "and" and "or" logic, while three of sixteen exhibit "left" or "right" logic.

The most startling result appeared with the conjoiner *dóó*. All of the information I could find before beginning the research said that the meaning of *dóó* was "and." Furthermore, bilingual consultants will consistently translate "and" to *dóó* and *dóó* to "and." Thus it came as a shock that in my tests *dóó* did not express "and" logic. Therefore I decided to check my results with a second "and" test.

In this test I elicited a truth table of English "and"-conjoined sentences from bilingual Navajos. The consultants then translated the sentences into Navajo, and I elicited a truth table of the Navajo sentences. If both my results and the translations of *dóó* in Navajo/English dictionaries were correct, I expected to see the logic change with the language. The English portions of the test would exhibit "and" logic, and the Navajo portions "right" logic (because both conjuncts of the Navajo version expressed perfective time). If my results were correct but the dictionary translations were incorrect, I expected to see "right" logic exhibited in both parts of the test. If my results were incorrect but the translations were correct, I expected to see "and" logic exhibited in both Navajo and English. Sentence (12) is the English test sentence.

(12) The gopher chased the mouse and bit the snake.

I elicited the truth tables independently from three male consultants ranging in age from 20 to 35 years old. Each English elicitation produced an "and" truth table. After eliciting the English truth tables, I asked each consultant to translate the sentences into Navajo. Sentence (13) is the translation given for sentence (12).

(13) *Na'asta'óósi na'azísí yinol'chéel dóó tł'iish yishhash.*

Then I elicited a truth table of the Navajo sentences; each consultant responded with "right" logic. These results increased my confidence in my findings.

Conclusions

These results show a complex interaction between the meanings of time markers and the meanings of conjoiners in Navajo compound sentences. The Navajo value on order, beauty, and harmony governs that interaction as well as Navajo subject pronouns. For example, neither the time marker study nor the subject pronoun study revealed conditional logic. This result can be explained by the fact that conditional reasoning is always ambiguous; to assert such reasoning is to create the disharmony that Navajo values seek to avoid.

In the Navajo view, time is circular. Changing Woman embodies this view. Most of the people that I talked to in the Rough Rock area, where I conducted the time marker study, did not consider her a Navajo but saw her as the mother of Monster Slayer and Child of the Water, the founders of Navajo culture. Other Navajo see her as the first Navajo, but all agree that she is young in the spring, matures through summer and fall to old age in the winter, and returns to youth in the spring. Some patterns of verb action, logic, and conjoiner meaning would break the cycle of time and produce chaos. Therefore the logic of each of these conjoiners changes as the pattern of verb action changes in the conjunct sentences.

For example, *biniinaa* shows two logics. It is "left" when the action of the right verb iterates, and it is "and" when the action either has ended or will end (the perfect and imperfect categories). Neither "left" nor "and" logics are true when the left conjunct is false. The "left" logic, however, can be true even if the right conjunct is false. Unlike the other conjoiners, *biniinaa* asserts a causal relationship between the left and the right conjuncts. The cause-effect relationship is true in the circle of time for terminal effects only when both cause and effect are true. When the effect repeats itself, the next cycle could manifest it again; the cause-effect relationship is true even when the effect is not apparent.

The logical changes in *éédoodaii'* are keyed to termination in the left conjunct verb action. Both *biniinaa* and *éédoodaii'* assert a left-to-right sequence, but *éédoodaii'* does not claim a causal relationship. Both exhibit "left" logic, but *biniinaa* is "left" when the right verb iterates, whereas *éédoodaii'* is "left" when the left sentence terminates. "Right" logic prevails when the left verb action iterates. In the case where the first element of a sequence can end, the circle of time requires a beginning. Therefore the first (left) conjunct defines the truth of the compound. On the other hand, when the first element of the sequence repeats itself, the series could begin on any iteration; thus harmony is created only when the second event occurs.

A sequence of events without cause also is asserted by *áádóó*. In this case, when the first event of the series has ended, *áádóó*, like *éédoodaii'*, exhibits "right" logic. On the other hand, when the action of the first verb is still in process (the imperfect categories), it shows either "left" or "and" logic. Where both verbs are in the imperfect mode, both verb actions must be true in order for the sequence to be orderly. Where the right verb action repeats, its next iteration could complete the sequence; in that case the left verb governs the compound's truth.

In these data *dóó* exhibits three logics: "or," "left," and "right."

Where the action of both verbs is complete, *dóó*, like *áádóó*, is "right" logic. Where the action of the second verb repeats itself, and therefore may change from false to true on its next iteration, order is created if either conjunct is true. Where both verb actions are still in process, order can result only when the first process is true. Thus, in the imperfect mode, *dóó* exhibits "left" logic.

The phenomenon of the logics of Navajo conjoiners changing with semantic aspects of the conjunct sentences is not unusual in human language. Recent research shows, for example, that the logics of "causes" and "if . . . then" change in English according to several semantic features of the conjunct sentences. In English such semantic features as necessary relatedness or abstractness of the conjunct sentences produce changes in logic (Staudenmayer 1975). In Navajo, time certainly acts in the same way. The finding that *dóó* does not express "and" logic, even though bilingual Navajos who understand the logical meaning of "and" translate it as "and," shows the need for further work in describing the patterns of Navajo reasoning.

Whorf, in his classic study of Hopi time, argued against the existence of what he called natural logic (Whorf 1964). The "natural logicians" of Whorf's time took the view that all human languages expressed a common logic; they maintained that the speaker's language described his or her world. The natural logicians said that the external world is a constant for any two people in the same place at the same time. Therefore descriptions of the same event that come from different languages are more or less equivalent. Whorf, on the other hand, believed that language actually categorized experience rather than simply describing the world. Thus two speakers of different languages would describe the same event in very different terms (Silverstein 1979:193–98). Whorf used Hopi syntactic time to make his point. He noted that the time expressed in Hopi sentences was not expressible, at least syntactically, in Indo-European languages. He concluded from this observation that the logic expressed in Hopi was different from that expressed in what he called Standard Average European. In other words, the same physical evidence does not lead speakers of different languages to the same conclusion.

The positivistic 1950s and 1960s were not kind to Whorf or to his proposition. In that era, researchers tried to test his ideas using highly restricted areas of language. Apparently these scholars reasoned that if the Whorfian hypothesis were not true for small areas of language, then it could not be true for language as a whole. The classic example of this research is Roger Brown and Eric Lennenberg's study of color terms (Brown and Lennenberg 1954). Their results showed that speakers of Navajo could distinguish the same color differences as speakers of English even though Navajo does not have separate terms for green and blue. Results such as these led many social scientists to disregard Whorf's ideas with perhaps too little consideration for the appropriateness of research.

In the same period, Quine took a view more congenial to Whorf's (Quine 1960:57–58). Quine described a scene with two people, one an English-speaking linguist and the other a speaker of a "hitherto untouched" language. They encounter what the linguist calls a rabbit. The non-English speaker points to the rabbit and says, "*Gavagai.*" Quine contended, in harmony with modern ethnosemantics, that one cannot conclude that "rabbit" translates exactly to *gavagai*. He asserted that the extensions of the terms, the class of things to which the terms refer, probably differ. That is, there is probably something that the English speaker calls "rabbit" that the other does not call *gavagai*. Also, there is something that the other calls *gavagai* that the English speaker does not call "rabbit." Quine then went beyond modern ethnosemantics, contending that even if the extensions of the two terms were identical, their intentions—the features and the combination of features that produce the class—probably would be different. That is, *gavagai* might denote a rabbit in position for shooting.

Quine differs from Whorf in his treatment of the translatability of logic. He contends that most classes of words (nouns and verbs) are not translatable but that logical connectors (and, or) are both translatable and universal. That is, Quine believes that there are direct translation equivalents of logical operators in all languages. The method he describes to find these equivalents is the principal method of this study.

The present findings show Quine to be wrong in some respects. Not only do we find no conditional ("if . . . then") patterns in Navajo; we cannot even find a word in Navajo that translates consistently to the logic of "and." We do find "and" logic with *biniinaa* and *áádóó*, but each of these conjoiners expresses "and" logic only in certain time pairings and expresses other logics when in other pairings. Thus "and" may not have a logical translation equivalent in Navajo. Sentences like (12) and (13) show us that the translation of logics is much more complicated than Quine would have us believe.

The semantic view of human reasoning fits well with these results. We see in Navajo much the same processes that Staudenmayer described in English: the internal semantics of sentences affect the logics they display. The semantics of Navajo time markers, however, are different from those of English; thus we observe different logics. Although this research does not weaken the idea of a meaning-based logic, it does little to support it, for the changes in logical patterns were documented but not explained. Unless the theory of semantically structured logic can produce the needed explanations, it must remain at the level of speculation.

Logical Processes in the General Theory of Culture 7

Culture is both meaning and process. It includes ways to assign and store meanings and the methods for manipulating them. If people could only collect meanings without using or changing them, then social life—indeed culture itself—would be stagnant and unchangeable. It would not be the fluid, adaptive, context-sensitive phenomenon that anthropologists describe in ethnographies. On the other hand, processes alone cannot describe culture at either the universal or the particular level. Processes are empty; they lack material or symbolic substance. People can and do modify processes, but they cannot function without substance. Together, meaning and process interact to produce new meanings and new processes; these make up the cultural diversity that anthropologists see around the world. At the same time, that diversity emerges from meanings and patterns of thought that all people share—that all people know. Because people learn their native culture through this knowledge, it is the general theory of culture.

What people do is one of the signs of these knowledge systems, but it is not the stuff of culture. Every act that we see is just one part of an activity stream. Most of this stream, however, is not open to direct observation. It matters very little that consultants often contradict in action the very rules they express in words. It is the task of ethnographers to resolve the contradictions in native terms using native processes. Ethnographers do well when they realize that the same underlying cultural order produces both the words and the deeds that contradict the words.

Anthropologists, and other scholars who seek to study the interaction of language, culture, and reasoning, face the difficult challenge of devising ways to ensure that the native is the source of everything. The problem is stubborn because we must observe from our point of view even though that very point of view limits what we think of as reasoning. It is necessary, therefore, to think about reasoning patterns in ways that will let the native define the reasoning system. I believe that semantic structures may be used to describe logical patterns in native terms. Future work in ethno-logic should test this and other ways to represent native logical systems until a conceptualization emerges that points to ways to capture native systems and to use data in ways that will preserve the integrity of the native patterns.

Because anthropologists have documented many different cultural orders, they have concluded that people acquire all of culture after birth through social interaction. When people acquire a culture they acquire a conceptual world, which includes the processes needed to manipulate it. These concepts and processes are knowledge, which is either innate or learned. The innate knowledge is the general theory of culture. The innate knowledge is universal; it is a property of all people. It is used to learn the distinct ways of life that people acquire; therefore all cultures are equally derivatives of it. The distinctiveness of these ways of life means that the basic nature of a particular culture is elaborated in the developmental process. Both the content and the patterns of thought are included in this elaboration. People learn both the terms by which they interpret their environment and the culturally appropriate ways to use those meanings. In short, enculturation means that people learn their culture through innate knowledge about what a culture is. The research into syllogistic and propositional reasoning patterns demonstrates this relationship clearly at both the theoretical and the descriptive levels.

Culture and Logic

The structure of categorical reasoning is the same regardless of language or culture. The results of all research into syllogistic reasoning have shown that when people reason with syllogisms, they draw conclusions validly. Furthermore, the pattern of valid and invalid syllogisms is the same from culture to culture and from language to language. This pattern differs from the one defined in logic textbooks because of differences in the meaning of the word "some." In the textbooks "some" means "there is one," whereas in natural language it means both "there is one" and "there is not one." Thus to say "Some trees are oaks" is also to say "Some trees are not oaks." In other words, "kind of" meanings link the terms in syllogisms. These terms also produce a logic that in some ways is more constrained than the textbook logic. The worldwide distribution of "kind of" meanings explains the worldwide distribution of valid syllogistic reasoning.

The research into propositional reasoning shows a more complex relationship between meaning and reasoning patterns. Both linguistic and cultural factors influence natives' judgments of the validity of propositionally expressed arguments. In English the logic of conditional sentences varies with the conjoiner used (because, if . . . then, etc.) and with the semantic relatedness and abstractness of the conjunct sentences. The truth-functional logic of Navajo compound sentences varies with the time markers and with the subject pronouns of the conjunct sentences. In these cases the meanings of the conjoiners, time markers, and pronouns are artifacts of the languages and culture in which they are found. Thus the logics exhibited in these sentences are also artifacts of language and culture.

Although the logics may differ from language to language, meanings always interact with structure to define validity. Consultants all over the world respond to syllogism tests in the same way because the "kind of" meaning is the principal component of syllogistic reasoning. Propositional patterns vary with language and culture because the semantic elements of the arguments mean different things in different settings. Those semantic differences can have both linguistic and cultural sources. For example, group consensus in political decision making is a strong cultural value among the Navajo. This value is strong in part because consensus contributes to Navajo judgments about whether an argument is good or bad. In a similar way, the time expressed by the various Navajo modes and aspects produces logical patterns that are distinctly Navajo. Thus the interaction of meaning and structure produces different logics in different settings.

Meaning not only structures validity in human thought patterns but also defines truth. Thus syllogisms are structured in the same way from culture to culture. Yet the inventory of true categorical statements varies with culture. Therefore it is possible for a valid conclusion to follow from a syllogism in one culture but to be false in another. Premises are a variable of culture in the same way as attributed causes. In western European culture, diseases are caused by microorganisms; in Navajo culture, disease is caused by disruptions in social harmony. Each culture labels the other culture's belief as false. Nonetheless, each belief participates as a true premise in validly patterned thought in their respective cultures. In other words, a culture provides both a theory of the universe and the cognitive tools with which to apply that theory. Anthropological theory is concerned with the symbolic structure of culture: how people acquire and use culture to adjust to real-time circumstances, and how people change those circumstances and their interpretations of them.

Theory and Culture

The most important development in any person's social life is the acquisition of culture. If culture could have infinite variety, the acquisition of culture could be explained easily with simple behavioral models. Such infinite variety is not the case, however; there is only a limited number of ways in which families are organized, political systems operate, and goods and services flow. These phenomena are not products of nature but of human nature. For example, many social systems, such as those of beehives and buffalo herds, do not include families; therefore families are not a necessary artifact of social life. No physical law of the universe, such as gravity, exists to define the structures and functions of social systems so that families result. Such structures and functions arise from the kind of animal that human beings are. Even so, various aspects of culture differ from one place to another. Thus culture varies and distinguishes one people from another, but only within a narrow range. A theory of culture should explain how people learn their culture; it also should explain why the culture they learn is so much like all others.

People acquire culture rapidly and with little formal training. By the age of seven most children have most of the knowledge they will use in life and know all the basic rules they need to participate in their community. These rules are abstract and complex; they involve activities as disparate and as complicated as language, appropriate posture, table manners, and dealings with kinspeople. Much of this acquired culture is subtle; even the learned adults in a culture often cannot state the rules that they are following.

By the age of seven, children have mastered a vast and intricate body of knowledge, mostly without being directly taught. It is true that adults often correct children, but they seldom teach them. Correction occurs only when the child has done something wrong, and even then it is applied inconsistently. Although correction always carries the message that the child has erred, it mentions only occasionally what the correct behavior should have been. Thus the child often is left alone to figure out the correct alternative. Children seem to do this easily, however. Adults almost never set out to teach a child some aspect of culture, having anticipated that he or she is ready to learn it. Under these conditions, the acquisition of culture can only be considered a monumental intellectual feat.

As a result of enculturation, people know how to act in their culture. This knowledge, however, cannot be merely a repertory of situations and the appropriate behaviors for them. As Blumer (1969:18) points out, almost all social situations are new. Even those that are repetitive must be created anew in each instance. If people could not act until they were able to identify their situation according to their existing knowledge and experience, they could not respond to any novel situation. In other words, people create culture on the spot through interaction with others. Anthropological theories of culture should incorporate this creativity into their explanations.

All people are essentially equal in their ability to become cultured, and all people encounter approximately the same amount of information in the process of enculturation. Thus it is untenable to maintain that one culture is "higher" or more complex than another. In reality, there are no simple or primitive cultures; all cultures are equally complex and equally modern.

Both the complexity of cultural knowledge and the creative use of this knowledge by native actors make it unlikely that people acquire culture through a stimulus-response system. Certainly behaviorists' models can account for some instances of learning, but behaviorist learning theories require the time-consuming repetition of stimulus, response, and reward. Therefore they cannot explain the acquisition of such a large amount of intricate knowledge in such a short time. Furthermore, the cultural knowledge learned through a stimulus-response regimen is a response to stimuli. It represents mechanical connections between input and output, situation, and behavior, and it cannot reflect the creativity that people actually exhibit.

The recent formulation of science as question asking (Laudan 1986) may be a more accurate metaphor for how people become cultured. In this model the child asks questions in two directions to develop a description of his or her culture—that is, to become enculturated. The child starts the process by making a statement that may or may not describe the culture. He or she checks the statement against the general theory of culture to see whether it is a possible description of any culture. If it is possible, the child then checks it against nature, through perception, to see whether the statement describes his or her culture. This procedure takes place tacitly; the child is no more aware of the processes of enculturation than of the processes of language acquisition.

What is true for the whole of culture is equally true for the thinking patterns that are part of it. Because meaning is part of the structure of reasoning, universally valid reasoning forms imply universal meanings that are not learned through experience. Rather, they are part of the general theory of culture and participate in the shaping of experience. The universality of the "kind of" semantic relationship explains the commonality of responses to syllogistic reasoning tests. The use of the "kind of" relationship in the symbol-processing part of culture is independently motivated by its universal use in the part of culture that catalogs meaning.

One cannot isolate meaning and logic from one another. If moving from meaning to action is a linear process, meanings do not structure logic. Let us say, for instance, that such a linear process involves three steps: (1) assigning a meaning to be expressed, (2) using that meaning as input to a logic processor, and (3) reaching a conclusion. The conclusion then is acted out. Here meaning has no path by which to modify the process that takes us from meaning to action; therefore meaning cannot modify logical patterns, nor can the results of reasoning create new meanings.

Meanings and processes must interact with one another and must be highly redundant. The logical behavior of Navajo compound sentences illustrates this point clearly. The truth-functional logic of Navajo sentences varies both with the subject pronouns and with the syntactic time markers used. In other words, the reasoning patterns express underlying cultural meanings and values. These results could not occur if reasoning and meaning did not interact. The logic must recognize the meanings that make up arrangements; the semantic component must identify logical features of meaning. Cultural meanings cannot be represented fully without reference to how they participate in reasoning patterns, nor can those patterns be represented without reference to the meanings they manipulate.

Current anthropological theories assume that culture emerges from some underlying cognitive base. Without such an assumption, symbolic anthropology would make little or no sense. Yet even supporters of the alleged antimentalist position taken in cultural materialism admit that culture grows out of underlying "bio-psychological" constraints. Without such constraints, cultural materialism could not explain "how infrastructure mediates between culture and nature" (Harris 1979:62). The overriding issue in anthropological theory is not whether theories of culture are mentalistic; all scholars agree that they are. The real debate is over the proper integration of material and mental phenomena.

Mental and Behavioral Data

A central focus of discussion in cultural materialism is the distinction between mental and behavioral events. Harris (1979:30–31) asserts that materialists must deal with this distinction in order to solve the problem of how to "achieve separate and valid scientific knowledge" of the material and the mental realms. Thus cultural materialism is not really antimentalistic; rather, it professes a proscientific rationale. It recognizes that thought is as real as matter and is a significant part of culture; therefore thought is properly a matter of concern to anthropological theory. Further, cultural materialism questions whether thought can be studied scientifically.

Harris posits that sociocultural systems have three major components, which are related through processes: the infrastructure, the structure, and the superstructure. Modes of production and reproduction make up the infrastructure. The structure is comprised of the political and the domestic economies. Two superstructures, etic and emic, consist of ideological rationalizations of the infrastructure and the structure. A linear process of probabilistic determination relates the components: the infrastructure determines the structure, which in turn determines the etic superstructure (Harris 1979:51–56). The emic superstructure consists entirely of mental phenomena and is set in opposition to the other three behavioral components. Therefore "mental" and "emic" are the same thing in cultural materialism because they occupy the same place in the theory.

All of Harris's examples of behavioral phenomena are actually examples of mental phenomena. For instance, technology, part of the infrastructure, does not simply comprise the tools that people make and how they use them. Rather, technology is what people know about making and using tools. The physical tools that people make and the behaviors that surround them are mere signs of the technology, not the technology itself. This is not to say that the behavioral manifestations of any component of cultural materialist theory are unimportant. On the contrary, they represent some of the most convincing evidence available about the form and structure of the various parts of culture. Yet to confuse infrastructural, structural, and superstructural behaviors with the knowledge that generates them is to confuse data with theory.

Cultural materialism is one of the best theories of culture in anthropology today. Materialists' accounts of social evolution and political-economic conflict are certainly among the most enlightening available. When materialism confuses knowledge with behavior, however, it limits its productivity unnecessarily. Infrastructure, structure, and superstructure are not universal components of sociocultural systems because they are imposed on people from the outside. These components, or something very much like them, are universal because they are part of the innate knowledge that forms the universal base of all culture.

In confusing behavioral with mental categories, cultural materialism reduces the contribution it can make to the understanding of enculturation. Materialism cannot explain why children easily learn the difference between tools and ritual items even when the same object has status in both categories. The child's acuity is explained easily, however, when the universal components of sociocultural systems are identified correctly. These components are not material phenomena but part of the knowledge that people use to acquire their culture.

If we accept the idea that infrastructure, structure, and superstructure all have a mental source, the priority of infrastructure in materialist theory becomes unwarranted. Infrastructural determinism is a research strategy; materialists adopted it because they regarded the behavioral infrastructure as the interface between culture and nature. The real interface, however, is the mind. In the mind, the organism uses knowledge to interact with and create the parameters of the environment. The infrastructure is no more or less the interface between nature and culture than are the structure and the superstructure. Furthermore, the processes that relate these components are not linear or one-directional. Infrastructure, structure, and superstructure feed and modify one another and exchange information. Materialist theory should both describe the meanings involved in this exchange and delimit the processes by which superstructure determines, and is determined by, infrastructure. More important, materialist theory should describe how infrastructure and superstructure participate in mutual creation and definition.

The Problem of Contradiction

A contradiction occurs when someone maintains that both "A" and "not A" are true in the same sense at the same time. In a contradictory universe, nothing has any meaning and anything can happen. Thus contradiction threatens to make any observed meaning system irrelevant. Harris (1979:271–78) uses this property of contradiction in his criticism of emic anthropology. Contradiction poses a problem in ethno-logic; it has the potential to destroy the meaning on which the descriptions of reasoning patterns rest. For the same reason it could create problems for any body of anthropological theory holding that meanings define culture.

If contradiction does not exist, it poses no threat to interpretive anthropology. That is, if people do not maintain contradictory ideas, the mere fact that we can imagine contradiction and even describe its structure has no bearing on symbolic, cognitive, or structural anthropology. People are not consistent; although they maintain contradiction, they also maintain meanings. Thus in the real world contradiction does not fulfill its logical threat to dissolve all meanings and to annihilate interpretive anthropology. It does, however, make it necessary for these theories to establish the processes that produce, shape, and limit contradiction. These processes should fulfill two theoretical functions: they should explain the presence of contradictions, and they should set the limits within which interpretive theory includes native contradiction.

Some years ago I tried to solve this problem by proposing that culture was organized in spheres of consistency (Hamill 1976). These spheres contain a few basic propositions and all of their derivatives. Consistency would rule within each sphere, but contradiction would be able to occur between spheres. Each of the spheres would be named with a traditional anthropological concept (infrastructure, structure, and superstructure).

Spheres of consistency explain nothing, however, because they merely describe metaphorically what must be the case if we accept that both meaning and contradiction are parts of human life. Furthermore, they do not do what I intended them to do: they place no limit on the amount of contradiction in culture, and they have no empirical motivation. There is no reason why there should be ten or fewer internally consistent meaning structures except for my desire to achieve simplicity. It would be more accurate to assume that contradictions, like meanings, are created and are therefore theoretically infinite in number.

These problems represent only one type of inadequate approach to contradiction in anthropological theory. Another approach relegates contradiction to ethnographic anomaly without offering an overarching ethnological explanation. For example, Douglas (1966: 140–58) observes that all social systems may contain contradiction. Unfortunately she uses this insight only to illustrate how social structures can produce contradictions.

The Mae Enga of highland Papua New Guinea and the Lele of central Africa, two groups that Douglas discusses extensively, represent good examples of structurally induced contradictions. Among the Mae Enga a rule of clan exogamy forces men to choose their wives from enemy clans. This rule produces a contradiction for the Mae Enga: among them, marriage is "built on enmity." As a result, Mae Enga men fear sexual pollution, practice elaborate purification rites, and avoid sexual contact with their wives.

In the case of the Lele, men compete with one another for prestige in the coin of women. Lele male dominance, however, does not extend to the right to coerce their wives and daughters. Thus Lele women hold the contradictory position of being both people and currency, and they play one man against another to their own advantage. The resulting Lele attitude toward sex is an ambivalent mixture of fear and pleasure, expressed by rules limiting the frequency of sexual intercourse and by purification rites performed by women on behalf of both sexes.

In these examples Douglas identifies an important source of contradiction in culture and describes some ways in which people deal with it, but she neither explains nor limits native contradiction. Her failure to treat contradiction at the theoretical level, on the one hand, and the "spheres of consistency" theory, on the other, define the basis on which a solution to the problem of contradiction can be proposed. Douglas is entirely correct; contradiction is an ethnographic fact. Thus no formulation of interpretive theory can include as a primitive of the theory the fact that people hold contradictory ideas. The fact of contradiction is data; as such, it must be a derivative of the theory. On the other hand, any theory from which the presence of contradiction follows must be independently motivated. It must explain important facts of social life other than contradiction.

Dynamic Interaction

In one very important way, interpretive anthropology has limited its potential for dealing productively with contradiction. Too often, anthropologists have viewed meaning as static, particularly in early cognitive anthropology, with its emphasis on folk taxonomies and paradigms. Of course, no one maintains that meaning is totally immutable; these schools of thought view cultural change as a change in meaning. Yet they also regard real-time behavior as a result of given meanings that do not change in particular social encounters. Rigid meaning can represent culture only partially and by itself cannot account for what people do. Almost all human acts are novel; even those that are repetitive must be created anew on each occasion.

Symbolic interaction theory, a branch of sociological theory, relies on a process of changing meaning. The proponents of this school of thought view social relations in terms of meanings that actors negotiate to establish their social realities. Individuals interact with others in this model through symbols whose meanings change as relationships progress. This idea can be applied to the problem of contradiction with productive results.

None of the symbols that people use to carry meaning are simple. By their very nature, symbols are complex bundles of meaning with many parts. I believe that people negotiate social realities by changing some of the component parts of symbols. Contradictions manifest themselves in terms of these components. If a person could come to a social interaction in a state of internal consistency, that interaction necessarily would produce contradiction. The interaction would change some of the meanings that were consistent with all of the other meanings held by the person, thus generating contradiction.

The same thing happens when the individual starts with contradiction. No meaning is ever totally inconsistent with all other meaning in a semantic system. If that were the case, that meaning would be no meaning. Thus even if some semantic feature contradicts another semantic feature within the system, it will be consistent with a third. In the process of social interaction, a change in one feature may produce a contradiction with a second feature, but it will resolve a contradiction with a third.

Thus the basic premise of symbolic interaction theory is that social life is a process of negotiated meaning. This approach solves some of the problems that contradiction creates for meaning-based theories of culture. According to this view, people generate contradictions and consistencies naturally as they interact with one another and create their social realities. In other words, contradiction is a derivative of the theory and has strong independent motivation.

People use what they know to create new meanings. They use the processes that are the core objects of ethno-logical study to create and use meanings. Some of those processes help to define our common humanity; they are universal and are used in all linguistic and cultural settings. Others help to define our membership in social groups. And processes used in one language and cultural setting may appear in another. Anthropologists have powerful tools at their disposal to study and learn about these processes. When researchers use these tools, the distinction between culture as symbol, meaning, or knowledge, and culture as act or behavior becomes clear.

References Cited

Agar, Michael H.
    1980   *The Professional Stranger*. New York: Academic Press.
    1986   *Speaking of Ethnography*. Beverly Hills, Calif.: Sage.
Andreski, Stanislav
    1972   *Social Science as Sorcery*. London: Andre Deutsch.
Barker, Stephen F.
    1965   *The Elements of Logic*. New York: McGraw-Hill.
Baugh, John, and Joel Sherzer
    1984   *Language in Use*. Englewood Cliffs, N.J.: Prentice-Hall.
Becker, Howard S.
    1958   Problems of Inference and Proof in Participant Observation. *American Sociological Review* 23(6): 652–60.
Berlin, Brent, Dennis Breedlove, and Peter H. Raven
    1973   General Principles of Classification and Nomenclature in Folk Biology. *American Anthropologist* 75:214–42.
Bloomfield, Leonard
    1926   A Set of Postulates for the Science of Linguistics. *Language* 2:153–64.
Blumer, Herbert
    1969   *Symbolic Interactionism*. Englewood Cliffs, N.J.: Prentice-Hall.
Boyle, Derek
    1982   Piaget and Education: A Negative Evaluation. In *Jean Piaget: Consensus and Controversy*, Sohan Modgil and Celia Modgil, eds., pp. 291–308. Lavenham: Lavenham Press Ltd.
Brown, Cecil H.
    1974   Unique Beginners and Covert Categories in Folk Biological Taxonomies. *American Anthropologist* 76:325–39.
    1976a Semantic Components, Meaning and Use in Ethnosemantics. *Philosophy of Science* 43:378–95.
    1976b General Principles of Human Anatomical Partonomy and Speculations on the Growth of Partonomic Nomenclature. *American Ethnologist* 3:400–424.
Brown, Roger, and Eric Lennenberg
    1954   A Study of Language and Cognition. *Journal of Abnormal and Social Psychology* 49:454–62.

Burling, Robins
   1964 Cognition and Componential Analysis: God's Truth or Hocus Pocus? *American Anthropologist* 66(1): 20–28.
Casagrande, Joseph, and Kenneth Hale
   1967 Semantic Relations in Papago Folk-Definitions. In *Studies in Southwestern Linguistics,* Dell Hymes and W. Bittle, eds., pp. 165–93. The Hague: Mouton.
Chagnon, Napoleon A.
   1983 *Yanomamo: The Fierce People.* 3d Ed. New York: Holt, Rinehart and Winston.
Chomsky, Noam
   1974 *Reflections on Language.* New York: Pantheon.
Churchland, Patricia Smith
   1980 A Perspective on Mind-Brain Research. *Journal of Philosophy* 17:185–207.
Churchland, Paul
   1984 *Matter and Consciousness: A Contemporary Introduction to the Philosophy of Mind.* Cambridge, Mass.: MIT Press.
Ciborowski, Thomas P., and Michael Cole
   1972 A Cross-Cultural Study of Conjunctive and Disjunctive Concept Learning. *Child Development* 43:474–89.
   1973 A Developmental and Cross-Cultural Study of the Influences of Rule Structure and Problem Composition on the Learning of Conceptual Classification. *Journal of Experimental Child Psychology* 15: 193–215.
Cole, Michael
   1973 A Developmental Study of Factors Influencing Discrimination Transfer. *Journal of Exceptional Child Psychology* 16:126–48.
   1985 The Zone of Proximal Development: Where Culture and Cognition Create Each Other. In *Culture, Communication, and Cognition: Vygotskian Perspectives.* James V. Wertsch, ed., pp. 146–61. Cambridge: Cambridge University Press.
Cole, Michael, John Gay, and Joseph Glick
   1968 A Cross-Cultural Investigation of Information Processing. *International Journal of Psychology* 3:93–102.
Cole, Michael, John Gay, Joseph Glick, and Donald W. Sharp
   1971 *The Cultural Context of Learning and Thinking.* New York: Basic Books.
Cole, Michael, and Sylvia Scribner
   1974 *Culture and Thought: A Psychological Introduction.* New York: Wiley.
   1975 Theorizing about Socialization of Cognition. *Ethos* 3(2):249–68.
D'Andrade, Roy Goodwin
   1981 The Cultural Part of Cognition. *Cognitive Science* 5:179–95.
Dennett, Daniel
   1978 *Brainstorms: Philosophical Essays on Mind and Psychology.* Montgomery, Vt.: Bradford.

Denzin, Norman K.
  1970 *The Research Act*. Chicago: Aldine.
Douglas, Mary
  1966 *Purity and Danger*. New York: Praeger.
Ervin-Tripp, Susan
  1972 On Sociolinguistic Rules: Alternation and Co-Occurrence. In *Directions in Sociolinguistics,* John Gumperz and Dell Hymes, eds., pp. 213–50. New York: Holt, Rinehart and Winston.
Evans-Pritchard, Edward Evan
  1937 *Witchcraft, Oracles and Magic among the Azandi*. Oxford: Clarendon.
Farella, John R.
  1984 *The Main Stalk: A Synthesis of Navajo Philosophy*. Tucson: University of Arizona Press.
Fodor, Jerry
  1975 *The Language of Thought: A Philosophical Study of Cognitive Psychology*. New York: Crowell.
Friedrich, Paul
  1986 *The Language Parallax: Linguistic Relativism and Poetic Indeterminacy*. Austin: University of Texas Press.
Gorman, Carl N.
  1973 Navajo Vision of Earth and Man. *The Indian Historian* 6(1): 19–22.
Greenberg, Joseph
  1963 Some Universals of Grammar with Particular Reference to the Order of Meaningful Elements. In *Universals of Language,* J. Greenberg, ed., pp. 73–113. Cambridge, Mass.: MIT Press.
Grize, Jean Glaise
  1967 Toward a Psycho-Logic. *Cahiers de Psychologie* 10:117–27.
  1979 One Aspect of Natural Logic: Contradiction in Discourse. *Bulletin de Psychologie* 32:655–64.
Gumperz, John
  1979 The Retrieval of Sociocultural Knowledge in Conversion. *Poetics Today* 1:273–86.
Gumperz, John, and Dell Hymes
  1972 *Directions in Sociolinguistics*. New York: Holt, Rinehart and Winston.
Hallpike, Christopher Robert
  1972 *The Konso of Ethiopia: A Study of the Values of a Cushitic People*. Oxford: Clarendon.
  1977 *Bloodshed and Vengeance in the Papuan Mountains: The Generation of Conflict in Tauade Society*. Oxford: Clarendon.
  1979 *The Foundations of Primitive Thought*. Oxford: Clarendon.
Hamill, James F.
  1976 Some Notes on a General Theory of Culture: A Possible Logical Constraint. Proceedings of the Central States Anthropological Society. Selected Papers 2:59–67.
  1979 Syllogistic Reasoning and Taxonomic Semantics. *Journal of Anthropological Research* 35:481–94.

Harris, Marvin
  1979 *Cultural Materialism: A Struggle for the Science of Culture.* New York: Random House.
Hempel, Carl
  1965 *Aspects of Scientific Explanation.* New York: The Free Press.
Hintikka, Jaakko
  1985 True and False Logics of Scientific Discovery. In *Logic of Discovery and Logic of Discourse,* Jaakko Hintikka and Fernand Vandamme, eds., pp. 3–14. New York: Plenum.
Hoijer, Harry
  1945 The Apachean Verb. Part I: Verb Structure and Pronominal Prefixes. *International Journal of American Linguistics* 11(4): 193–203.
Hughes, Everett C.
  1951 Mistakes at Work. *Canadian Journal of Economics and Political Science* 17: 320–27.
Hutchins, Edwin
  1980 *Culture and Inference: A Trobriand Case Study.* Cambridge, Mass.: Harvard University Press.
Kay, Paul
  1975 A Model-Theoretic Approach to Folk Taxonomy. *Social Science Information* 14(5): 151–66.
Kay, Paul, and Willett Kempton
  1984 What Is the Sapir-Whorf Hypothesis? *American Anthropologist* 86: 65–79.
Kempton, Willett
  1978 Category Grading and Taxonomic Relations: A Mug Is a Sort of Cup. *American Ethnologist* 5: 44–65.
Kluckhohn, Clyde, and Dorothea Leighton
  1962 *The Navajo.* Garden City, N.Y.: Doubleday.
Kuhn, Thomas
  1962 *The Structure of Scientific Revolutions.* Chicago: University of Chicago Press.
Laudan, Larry
  1986 Some Problems Facing Intuitionist Meta-Methodologies. *Synthese* 67: 115–29.
Lévi-Strauss, Claude
  1966 *The Savage Mind.* Chicago: University of Chicago Press.
Lévy-Bruhl, Lucien
  1926 *How Natives Think.* New York: Knopf.
  1975 *The Notebooks on Primitive Mentality.* Oxford: Basil Blackwell.
Lewis, George H., and Jonathan Lewis
  1980 The Dog in the Night-Time: Negative Evidence in Social Research. *British Journal of Sociology* 31: 544–58.
Luria, A. R.
  1971 Towards the Problem of the Historical Nature of Psychological Processes. *International Journal of Psychology* 6: 259–72.
  1979 *The Making of Mind.* Cambridge, Mass.: Harvard University.

Malinowski, Bronislaw
- 1922 *Argonauts of the Western Pacific.* London: Routledge.

McKenna, William B.
- 1986 What Can Anthropology Contribute to Logic and What Can Logic Contribute to Anthropology? Paper presented at the annual meeting of the Central States Anthropological Society.

McNeley, James Kale
- 1981 *Holy Wind in Navajo Philosophy.* Tucson: University of Arizona Press.

Pelto, Pertti
- 1970 *Anthropological Research: The Structure of Inquiry.* New York: Harper and Row.

Piaget, Jean, Jean Blaise Grize, Alina Szemiska, and Bang Vinh
- 1977 *Epistemology and Psychology of Functions.* Boston: Reidel.

Pinxten, Rik, Ingrid van Dooren, and Frank Harvey
- 1983 *The Anthropology of Space: Explorations into the Natural Philosophy and Semantics of the Navajo.* Philadelphia: University of Pennsylvania Press.

Quine, Willard V.
- 1960 *Word and Object.* Cambridge, Mass.: MIT Press.
- 1986 *Philosophy of Logic.* Cambridge, Mass.: Harvard University Press.

Reichard, Gladys
- 1950 *Navajo Religion: A Study of Symbolism.* Princeton: Princeton University Press.

Reichenbach, Hans
- 1947 *Elements of Symbolic Logic.* New York: Free Press.

Riemer, Jeffrey W.
- 1976 "Hard Hats" Mistakes at Work—The Social Organization of Error in Building Construction Work. *Social Problems* 23:255–67.

Ross, John
- 1970 Gapping and the Order of Constituents. In *Progress in Linguistics,* Manfred Bierwisch and Karl Heidolph, eds., pp. 249–59. The Hague: Mouton.

Russell, Bertrand
- 1940 *An Inquiry in Meaning and Truth.* New York: Norton.

Schieffelin, Bambi B.
- 1984 Ade: A Sociolinguistic Analysis of a Relationship. In *Language in Use,* John Baugh and Joel Sherzer, eds., pp. 229–44. Englewood Cliffs, N.J.: Prentice-Hall.

Schoepfle, Mark, Michael Burton, and Frank Morgan
- 1984 Navajos and Energy Development: Economic Decision Making under Political Uncertainty. *Human Organization* 43:265–72.

Scribner, Sylvia
- 1975 Recall of Classical Syllogisms: A Cross-Cultural Investigation of Errors on Logical Problems. In *Reasoning: Representation and Process,* Rachel Falmagne, ed., pp. 153–74. Hillsdale, N.J.: Lawrence Erlbaum.

Scribner, Sylvia, and Michael Cole
 1972 Effects of Constrained Recall Training on Children's Performance on a Memory Task. *Child Development* 43:845–57.
 1978 Unpackaging Literacy. *Social Science Information* 17(1):19–40.
 1981 *The Psychology of Literacy.* Cambridge, Mass.: Harvard University Press.
Sharp, Donald, Michael Cole, and Charles Lave
 1978 Education and Cognitive Development: The Evidence from Experimental Research. *Monographs of the Society for Research in Child Development* 44(1–2):1–12.
Silverstein, Michael
 1979 Language Structure and Linguistic Ideology. In *The Elements: A Session on Linguistic Units and Levels,* Paul R. Clyne, William F. Hanks, and Carol L. Hofbauer, eds., pp. 193–247. Chicago: Chicago Linguistic Society.
Sjoberg, Gideon, and Roger Nett
 1968 *A Methodology for Social Research.* New York: Harper and Row.
Skinner, B. F.
 1953 *Science and Human Behavior.* New York: Macmillan.
Spradley, James P.
 1981 *Participant Observation.* New York: Holt, Rinehart and Winston.
Staudenmayer, Herman
 1975 Understanding Conditional Reasoning with Meaningful Propositions. In *Reasoning: Representation and Process,* Rachel Falmagne, ed., pp. 55–80. Hillsdale, N.J.: Lawrence Erlbaum.
Tomlinson-Keasey, Carol
 1982 Structures, Functions and Stages: A Trio of Unresolved Issues in Formal Operations. In *Jean Piaget: Consensus and Controversy,* Sohan Modgil and Celia Modgil, eds., pp. 131–53. Lavenham: Lavenham Press Ltd.
Tyler, Stephen A.
 1969 *Cognitive Anthropology.* New York: Holt, Rinehart and Winston.
Vogt, Evon
 1961 Navajo. In *Perspectives in American Indian Culture Change,* E. Spicer, ed., pp. 278–337. Chicago: University of Chicago Press.
Waldrop, M. Mitchell
 1987 *Man-Made Minds: The Promise of Artificial Intelligence.* New York: Walker.
Weizenbaum, Joseph
 1976 *Computer Power and Human Reason: From Judgment to Calculation.* San Francisco: Freeman.
Werner, Oswald, and G. Mark Schoepfle
 1987 *Systematic Fieldwork.* Beverly Hills, Calif.: Sage.
Werner, Oswald, and Martin Topper
 1976 On the Theoretical Unity of Ethnoscience Lexicography and Ethnoscience Ethnography. In *Semantics: Theory and Application,* Clea

Rameh, ed., pp. 111–43. Washington, D.C.: Georgetown University Press.

Wertsch, James V.
1985 *Culture, Communication, and Cognition: Vygotskian Perspectives.* Cambridge: Cambridge University Press.

Whitehead, Alfred North, and Bertrand Russell
1910 *Principia Mathematica.* Cambridge: Cambridge University Press.

Whorf, Benjamin Lee
1964 Science and Linguistics. In *Language, Thought and Reality,* John Carol, ed., pp. 207–19. Cambridge, Mass.: MIT Press.

Witherspoon, Gary
1977 *Language and Art in the Navajo Universe.* Ann Arbor: The University of Michigan Press.

Young, Robert W., and William Morgan
1980 *The Navajo Language: A Grammar and Colloquial Dictionary.* Albuquerque: University of New Mexico Press.

Index

Aadoo, 78, 81, 95, 98, 100
Agar, Michael H., 51, 58, 113
Ago, 32
Ako, 78
Ambiguity, 45
Andreski, Stanislav, 14, 113
Anomaly, 45, 51, 110
Anthropology: cognitive, 9, 37, 61, 109, 111; interpretive, 109–111; symbolic, 104, 107, 109
Asbob, 33

Barker, Stephen F., 62, 70, 81, 113
Baugh, John, and Joel Sherzer, 12, 113, 117
Becker, Howard S., 50, 56, 113
Berlin, Brent, Dennis Breedlove, and Peter H. Raven, 61, 113
biniinaa, 95, 98, 100
Bloomfield, Leonard, 13, 113
Blumer, Herbert, 105, 113
Boyle, Derek, 10, 11, 113
Breakdowns, 51
Brown, Cecil, 61, 113
Brown, Roger, and Eric Lenninberg, 99, 113
Burling, Robins, 61, 114

Casagrande, Joseph, and Kenneth Hale, 20, 42, 114
Category, complexive, 32
Chagnon, Napoleon, 51, 114
Chidí, 73
Chomsky, Noam, 9, 114
Churchland, Patricia Smith, 9, 114
Churchland, Paul, 9, 114
Class inclusion, 16, 17, 20, 37, 60–62, 74, 75
Cognitive science, 5, 9, 19, 26
Cole, Michael, 11, 29–32, 34–38, 40, 50, 60, 61, 70, 76, 114, 118

Conjunction, 75, 81, 85
Consistency, 12, 13, 23, 25; spheres of, 110–12
Constituents: order of, 52, 53
Contradiction, 25–27, 109–12
Creativity, 8, 13–14, 49, 106
Cultural particulars, xi, 3, 4, 6–7, 16, 20–21, 39, 44, 57, 59, 102
Cultural universals, xi, 3, 4, 6–7, 12, 18–21, 37, 40, 41, 42, 46, 49, 55, 102, 106–9, 112
Culture:
—Anglo, xiii, 6, 7, 88
—Azandi, 51
—Bororo, 26
—general theory of, 2–3, 6–7, 21, 47, 57–58, 102, 106, 108
—Hopi, 27, 28, 99
—indigenous, 36
—Konso, 29–32
—Kpelle, 30, 34–36
—Kwii, 35
—Lele, 110, 111
—Mae Enga, 110
—Mexican, 30
—Navajo, xii, xiii, 2–4, 6, 7, 16, 20, 21, 37–39, 41, 60, 66, 68, 70, 73–81, 83–94, 96–100, 104, 107
—primitive, 4, 13, 16, 25–28, 30, 39, 40, 106
—Tauade, 29, 30, 32
—Trobriand, 29–31
—Vai, 30, 34, 36

Da:k, 42
D'Andrade, Roy Goodwin, 9, 12, 114
Dennett, Daniel, 9, 114
Denzin, Norman K., 50, 115
Diégó, 78, 81, 87
Dirt, 45, 47, 48, 52
Discourse, 16, 24, 43, 75

122 Index

Disjunction, 35, 75, 85, 87, 88
Disorder in Navajo worldview, 85–86
Doo, 96–97, 98–99
Doo . . . da, 80
Douglas, Mary, 45, 47, 48, 50, 52, 110, 111, 115

Éédoodaii', 78, 81, 85, 87–88, 95, 98
Enculturation, 57, 103, 105, 106, 109
Ervin-Tripp, Susan, 12, 115
Ethnography, 13, 15, 25, 26, 30–34, 50–51
Evans-Pritchard, Edward Evan, 51, 115
Evidence, 50–51, 86–87

Farella, John R., 86, 115
Figures, syllogism, 63, 64, 66, 68
Folk taxonomies, 20, 37, 61, 62, 111
Fodor, Jerry, 9, 115
Frames, 20, 64
Friedrich, Paul, 28, 115
Fuzzy sets, 62

Gapping, xii, 52–55
Gorman, Carl N., 88, 115
Grammar, 24, 27–28, 54
Greenberg, Joseph, 17, 115
Grize, Jean Glaise, 24, 115, 117
Gumperz, John, 12, 115

Hallpike, Christopher Robert, 29–32, 115
Harris, Marvin, 10, 13, 22, 46, 107–9, 116
Hempel, Carl, 86, 116
Hintikka, Jaakko, 24, 116
Hoijer, Harry, 79, 116
Hózhó, 85, 86
Hughes, Everett C., 50–52, 116
Hutchins, Edwin, 29–31, 116

Infrastructure, 22, 46, 49, 107–9, 110
Interpretation, 8, 11, 37, 55
Intracultural variation, 56, 59

Kay, Paul, 20, 28, 62, 116
Kempton, Willett, 28, 62, 116
Kluckhohn, Clyde, and Dorothea Leighton, 85, 116
Knowledge, 8–12, 18, 19, 22, 31, 36, 37, 44–52, 55–59, 102–3, 105–6, 108–9, 112, 115; innate, 1–3, 4, 6, 11, 46–47, 49, 52, 57, 102–3
Kuhn, Thomas, 86, 116

Language:
—Algonquian, 37, 60
—Arabic, 36
—Athabascan, 37, 60, 73, 74
—English, 3, 4, 21, 28, 36, 37, 39, 41, 47, 53, 60, 66, 68, 70, 75, 76, 77, 82–83, 92, 93, 94, 97, 99, 100–101, 104
—general theory of, 1–2, 4, 5, 8–9, 11–13, 16, 17–18, 19, 24, 27–28, 38–41, 43, 45, 46–49, 52–55, 59–61, 70–72, 85, 88–89, 90, 94, 99, 100, 102–4, 106, 112
—Indo-European, 37, 55, 60, 99
—Japanese, 52–53
—Mande-kan, 37, 60
—Mayan, 30
—Mende, xiii, 3, 37–39, 60, 66–68, 70
—Navajo, xii, xiii, 2, 3–4, 6, 7, 20–21, 37–39, 41, 60, 66, 68, 70, 73–101, 104, 107
—Ojibwa, xiii, 3, 37, 39, 60, 66, 68, 70
—Papago, 42, 114
—Russian, 53
—Uzbekhi, 33
Language acquisition device, 2, 12, 46
Laudan, Larry, 86, 106, 116
Lévi-Strauss, Claude, 23, 116
Lévy-Bruhl, Lucien, 16, 26–29, 116
Lewis, George H., and Jonathan Lewis, 50, 116
Literacy, 3, 4, 5, 11, 25, 34, 36, 70, 76
Logic:
—Aristotelian, 15, 16
—biconditional, 82, 86, 87
—categorical, 6, 33, 39, 72, 103, 104
—conditional, 78, 81–87, 96, 97, 100, 104
—conjunctive, 80, 81
—disjunctive, 83–85, 88
—empirical, 18, 23, 24, 36
—formal, 4, 12, 14, 24, 61
—and implication, 35
—linear, 107
—philosophical, 5, 6, 15, 18–20
—primitive, 4, 5, 13, 16, 25–28, 30, 31, 39

—propositional, xii, 4, 6, 7, 11, 16–18, 20, 21, 40, 41, 60, 72, 74, 75, 77, 90, 94, 103, 104
—and semantic relatedness, 75, 77, 80, 81, 83, 99, 104
—syllogistic, xii, 6, 11, 15–16, 17, 19–21, 25, 29, 32–33, 34–41, 59, 60–72, 74–75, 103, 104, 107
—textbook, 3, 6, 18, 20, 23–25, 31, 37, 39–40, 59– 61, 63–66, 71, 73, 103
Logical operators, 6, 17, 20, 40, 75, 90, 100
Luria, A. R., 11, 29–35, 37, 38, 40, 60, 61, 70, 76, 116

Malinowski, Bronislaw, 10, 56, 117
McKenna, William, 18, 117
McNeley, James Kale, 86, 117
Methods, xii, 5, 6, 14, 17–20, 25, 30–32, 37, 45, 49–51, 56, 58, 59, 60, 61, 63, 75, 76, 85, 90–91, 93, 100, 102
—ethnographic, 15, 25, 31, 33, 34, 50–51, 56–57, 102
—field, 50–51, 57–59, 61
—participant observation, 25, 56, 58
—psychometric, 26, 30, 34
—qualitative, 50, 58
—quantitative, 50

Negation: logical, 23, 71–72, 81; syntactic, 80

Observability, 13–14

Paradigm: data elicitation, 21, 43, 50, 51, 74–81, 91–92; scientific, 86, 87
Pelto, Pertti, 51, 117
Perception, 28, 90, 106
Piaget, Jean, 10, 11, 24, 61, 113, 117, 118
Pinxten, Rik, Ingrid van Dooren, and Frank Harvy, 86, 117
Political systems: consensus, 6, 73, 74, 88, 104, 113, 118; egalitarian, 73, 74, 88
Pollution, 47, 110
Prelogical mentality, 26, 27, 29, 39
Premise, 17, 71, 72, 75, 78, 104, 112; major, 16, 34, 36, 38–39, 62–64, 68, 77, 79–80, 82–84, 86, 87; minor, 16, 38, 39, 62–64, 68, 77, 79, 80

Propositions: data elicitation, 74, 75, 77, 79–81, 83, 84, 87
Protocol, 37, 43, 62, 64
Psychology, 9, 15, 26, 29–31, 36; developmental, 18, 24, 25; experimental, 30

Quine, Willard V., 12, 17, 20, 24, 93, 100, 117

Reality, 10, 22, 45
Reichard, Gladys, 86–88, 117
Representation, 61–62
Riemer, Jeffery W., 50, 52, 117
Role, 57
Ross, John, xii, 52–55, 117
Rules, 5–6, 9, 20, 23, 39, 53–54, 57, 59, 62, 63, 70–72, 75, 79, 85, 88, 102, 105
Russell, Bertrand, 16, 17, 61, 117, 119

Schieffelin, Bambi B., 12, 117
Schoepfle, Mark, 12, 20, 31, 37, 42, 51, 56
Scribner, Sylvia, 11, 29–31, 34, 36, 76, 114, 117, 118
Semantic(s), 28, 71, 84, 89, 92, 100; domains, 30, 36, 64–67; logical, 5, 40–43, 49, 64–67, 72, 74–75, 77, 80–83, 87, 88, 90–92, 94, 99, 100, 101, 103, 104, 106–7; taxonomic (kind of), 6, 7, 20, 21, 37, 39–43, 61–62, 64–67, 71–72, 106–7
Silverstein, Michael, 28, 99, 118
Sjoberg, Gideon, and Roger Nett, 50, 118
Skinner, B. F., 13, 118
Spradley, James P., 20, 42, 51, 56, 118
Staudenmayer, Herman, 72, 82, 94, 99, 100, 118
Structure, xii, 2–3, 5–7, 11, 14, 17–18, 19, 21, 28, 39–41, 43, 45, 49, 55–56, 59, 69–70, 71–72, 74, 76–77, 90, 101, 103–4, 106–7
Superstructure, 22, 46, 108–10

Taboo, 47–48
Theory:
—behavioral, 88, 105–6
—colonial, 13, 28–30, 36
—conflict, 22, 24, 45
—cultural materialism, 10, 46, 107–9, 116

Theory (*continued*)
—ethnosemantic, 12, 40, 41, 61
—external, 45, 48, 49, 51
—French structuralism, 56
—functionalism, 10, 22, 24, 45
—interpretive, 109–11
—learning, 2, 29, 34, 57, 58, 106
—Piagetian, 11, 30
—psychological, 24, 25, 29, 34
—sociological, 22, 45–46, 56, 111
—symbolic interaction, 111–12
—transformational-generative, 1, 2, 4, 5, 9, 19, 45, 47, 52, 55
—Vygotskian, 11, 31, 76
—Whorfian, 27–28, 99–100
Thinking: as reasoning, xii, 2–6, 13, 19, 24, 27, 29, 33, 34, 40, 59, 61, 76, 106; paradigmatic, 33; pre-operative, 31–32, 39

Tomlinson-Keasey, Carol, 11, 118
Tyler, Stephen A., 61, 118

Validity, xi–xii, 6, 7, 13, 15–17, 19–21, 39–40, 43, 45, 59, 60, 63–66, 68–72, 74, 75, 81–82, 90, 103–4
Vogt, Evon, 73, 118

Waldrop, M. Mitchell, 9, 118
Weizenbaum, Joseph, 9, 118
Werner, Oswald, xiii, 12, 20, 31, 37, 42, 51, 56, 62, 118
Wertsch, James V., 76, 114, 119
Whorf, Benjamin Lee, 26–28, 99, 100, 116, 119
Witherspoon, Gary, 85, 86, 119

Young, Frank, and William Morgan, 79, 98, 119

Note on the Author

James F. Hamill is Assistant Professor of Anthropology at Miami University, Oxford, Ohio. He received his Ph.D. from the University of Wisconsin-Milwaukee in 1974. Hamill has been published in scholarly journals ranging from *Symbolic Interaction* to *Anthropological Linguistics* to the *Journal of Anthropological Research*. *Ethno-Logic: The Anthropology of Human Reasoning* is his first published book.